577273

382 BER

¡ONE WEEK LOAN

KT-458-704

On the Brink of Deglobalization

It is a capital mistake to theorize before one has data. Insensibly one begins to twist facts to suit theories, instead of theories to suit facts.

Penguin Complete Sherlock Holmes, 1981, p. 163

Cover illustration based on Peeter Burgeik, 'Collapsing web of trade', 2010, etch and lithograph, printed on the KARL KRAUSE press at Steendrukkerij Aad Hekker, Amsterdam. The source of inspiration is Kindleberger's (1973, p. 172) 'spider web' diagram of the contracting spiral of world trade.

On the Brink of Deglobalization

An Alternative Perspective on the Causes of the World Trade Collapse

Peter A.G. van Bergeijk

Professor of International Economics/Macroeconomics, International Institute of Social Studies of Erasmus University, The Hague, and CERES Research School for Resource Studies for Development, Utrecht University, The Netherlands

Edward Elgar
Cheltenham, UK • Northampton, MA, USA

© Peter A.G. van Bergeijk 2010

All rights reserved. No part of this publication may be reproduced, stored in a retrieval system or transmitted in any form or by any means, electronic, mechanical or photocopying, recording, or otherwise without the prior permission of the publisher.

Published by
Edward Elgar Publishing Limited
The Lypiatts
15 Lansdown Road
Cheltenham
Glos GL50 2JA
UK

Edward Elgar Publishing, Inc.
William Pratt House
9 Dewey Court
Northampton
Massachusetts 01060
USA

A catalogue record for this book
is available from the British Library

Library of Congress Control Number: 2010927666

SC.................OLENT
UNIVERSITY LIBRARY
SUPPLIER Blacc〕
ORDER No
DATE 21-10-10

ISBN 978 1 84980 411 0 (cased)

Printed and bound by MPG Books Group, UK

Contents

Preface and Acknowledgements

In February 2009 I started in a new job as a professor of international economics and macroeconomics. It could not have been a more timely appointment for me because one of the major intellectual challenges for the subject field of international economics was well underway. Not many people were actually worrying about the risky developments of world trade at that moment, although some already speculated on this topic of course. So did I when I was commenting on the launch of the OECD's *Development Co-operation Report 2009* on February 18, 2009 at the premises of the Institute of Social Studies in The Hague: 'We do not have the data yet, but we can try to glean beyond the report at what is happening and what this means. It is to be expected that low income earners will be hit hardest and especially in countries where no social security safety nets exist. Developing countries that opened up to the world economy are now experiencing the down side of strategies that – for good reasons – relied on international trade and foreign direct investment to achieve national development. Presently international trade volumes are collapsing and foreign direct investment decisions are probably being postponed if not cancelled as a consequence of the credit crisis. Also other sources of foreign finance will dry up: remittances from expatriates, bank lending, and portfolio investment will in all likelihood not provide a leeway.'

Early April 2009 I started the research project on the world trade collapse on which this book is based. At that time one could still only hypothesize that trade would become a casualty of the financial crisis because the available data sources – with the exceptions of the *CPB World Trade Monitor* (that had been launched on March 20, 2009) and the so-called 'Baltic dry index' (that tracks worldwide international shipping prices) – did not yet provide indications of the very strong trade collapse that we know now was taking place at that moment. I started the project in order to have something interesting to tell in my inaugural lecture 'I come to bury globalization, not to praise it' for which I had set the date at October 29, 2009, eighty years after the Wall Street Crash. With hindsight it was a perfect date: it also appeared to be the first anniversary of the start of the world trade collapse

This book is a low pretence exercise that only aims to make a scientific but still very preliminary assessment of recent contributions to the literature. It attempts to distil some of the empirical regularities that are emerging in data that will be updated and revised over the next quarters if not months. Perhaps someone would want to object that it is much more scientific to wait longer and then make a better, more precise and perhaps less uncertain analysis. I also do not develop a formal model but work with descriptive statistics and simple quasi-postulated reduced form equations that in a very common sense approach take account of some of the explanations for the world trade collapse that have been floated in the literature. Also this lack of formal structure may attract criticism from academia. For a preliminary assessment, however, the methodology suffices. Such a preliminary assessment in my opinion is much needed: the problems posed by the world trade collapse are too serious to take the intellectual luxury to wait for the perfect analysis.

ACKNOWLEDGEMENTS

The first research output of the project was published in Dutch on May 1, 2009 in *Economisch Statistische Berichten* (an English version of that article appears in the November 2009 issue of *Kyklos*) and these articles – updated and amended – form the basis for Chapter 2. I benefitted from the comments by the editors and referees. I was also helped because I could present the ideas in this book in raw shape at a number of workshops and seminars. I would like to thank the organizers and discussants at these meetings, in particular ECORYS in Rotterdam (April 16, 2009), Groningen University (September 14, 2009), the HIVOS strategy meeting in Noordwijk (September 17, 2009), ISS's Research in Progress (October 1, 2009), CPB Netherlands Bureau for Economic Analysis (October 13, 2009) and VNO-NCW (November 12, 2009). Steven Brakman and Karel Jansen were very critical and helpful in commenting on a first draft of the manuscript. I would also like to thank my students, especially those attending courses 4207 and 4312 at ISS and the students of BOFEB where I had a try-out of ideas for a very critical public.

Box 1.1 appears by permission of the World Trade Organisation. Figures 2.4 and 2.6 appear by permission of the Asian Development Bank. Figure 4.5 appears by kind permission of Charles van Marrewijk. Appendix 1A.1 is partially based on van Bergeijk and Mensink (1997) and appears by permission of the *Journal of World Trade*.

Nieuw Vennep,
March 2010

1. Introduction: Setting the Stage

October 2008 had something extraordinary in store for globalization. In the years 2004–2008 the world trade volume had been growing at an annual rate of between 5 and 10 per cent. These were high numbers but they were not outside the usual range for the development of real exports and imports at the global level – world trade over the period 1950–2008 grew by about 6 per cent per annum leading to a 25-fold increase in the volume of merchandise trade. In October 2008 world trade, however, suddenly came to a virtual halt and then started to decline. This decline rapidly turned into a collapse. In November 2008 the global trade volume declined by 7 per cent. December 2008 added 3 per cent; January 2009 another 7 per cent: early 2009 trade figures were about 20 per cent lower in real terms than they had been just one year earlier (Figure 1.1).

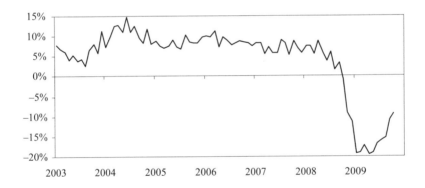

Source: CPB world trade monitor at www.cpb.nl

Figure 1.1   Growth rate of world trade with respect to same month in the previous year (2003–2009)

In the second half of 2009 some recovery occurred. According to the December 2009 issue of the CPB *World Trade Monitor*: 'In October, world trade was still 13.2% below the peak level reached in April 2008 mainly resulting from the unprecedented drops in November 2008 up to January

2009. Compared to [2008] world trade was down by 9.4% in October, but it was already 9.0% above the trough reached in May 2009'.

This book deals with the collapse of trade and not so much with its recovery. It is not a study on the full 'business cycle' of trade as it focuses on the downturn (and its potential continuation) and the lessons that this exceptional 'natural experiment' provide for economic scientists and policy makers. The main narrative for this phenomenon is that the world trade collapse was caused by the collapses of (i) trade credit, (ii) international value chains and (iii) the multilateral policy approach to free trade (an increase in protectionism). This book will clarify that this theory for the world trade collapse collapses when confronted with the data. Focussing on the development of import volumes, I suggest an alternative explanation, namely that the trade collapse was driven by a shock of (perceived) trade uncertainty and provide some preliminary evidence for this hypothesis.

Typically, the mainstream analysis is based on preconceptions about what the drivers of the trade collapse should be. This book challenges the mainstream narrative of the world trade collapse because that narrative is wrong and because it provides the wrong kind of policy advice, thus increasing the risk of a deepening and prolongation of the crisis in international trade. Even when the mainstream explanations are refuted by data analysis, authors often stick to the idea that theory must somewhere be right and that the data must somewhere be wrong. The latter may be right but the former is a *non sequitur* or at least a very *non-empirical* argument. The fact that data are imperfect most of the time, only available with substantial delay and often do not exist, however, to a large extent could explain why many wrong ideas are able to survive for so long. The bottom line is that the economic profession does not offer a convincing explanation yet.

Admittedly, the profession, in particular the economists at the international institutions, has provided a long list of potential explanations, but we are far away from a real understanding of the 2008–2009 trade collapse.[1] This will become evident when we scrutinize in later chapters the explanations on the long list that the World Trade Organization put forward in its *World Trade Report 2009* (WTO 2009b, p. 2 and p. 18). The WTO suggests six explanations for the strength of the trade collapse: the decrease of commodity prices, swings in the value of the US dollar, the concurrence of problems in all countries, the occurrence and intensity of global supply chains, shortage of trade finance, and an increase in protectionism. The other organizations have echoed the WTO's long list which appears to have had a strong intuitive appeal, often stressing some of the factors that in particular relate to their respective missions.

The WTO's analysis is especially noteworthy because it is rather disappointing. This is true for the quantity of the reported analysis (which covers one half of a page – out of a report with a total of 196 pages – and one footnote). It is also true for the quality of the analysis as many of the listed 'explanations' actually are logically flawed and have potentially dangerous policy conclusions as we will see in later chapters.[2]

Box 1.1 Factors explaining the extent of the world trade collapse according to the WTO's World Trade Report 2009

One reason is that the fall-off in demand is more widespread than in the past, as all regions of the world economy are slowing at once.

A second reason for the magnitude of recent declines relates to the increasing presence of global supply chains in total trade. Trade contraction or expansion is no longer simply a question of changes in trade flows between a producing country and a consuming country – goods cross many frontiers during the production process and components in the final product are counted every time they cross a frontier. The only way of avoiding this effect, whose magnitude can only be guessed at in the absence of systematic information, would be to measure trade transactions on the basis of the value added at each stage of the production process. Since value added, or the return to factors of production, is the real measure of income in the economy, and trade is a gross flow rather than a measure of income, it follows that strong increases or decreases in trade flow numbers should not be interpreted as an accurate guide to what is actually happening to incomes and employment.

A third element that is likely to contribute to the contraction of trade is a shortage of trade finance. This has clearly been a problem and it is receiving particular attention from international institutions and governments. The WTO has played its part by bringing together the key players to work on ensuring the availability and affordability of trade finance.

A fourth factor that could contribute to trade contraction is an increase in protection measures. Any rises in these measures will threaten the prospects for recovery and prolong the downturn. The risk of growing protectionism is a source of concern.*

*   Two factors that might accentuate the extent of year-on-year declines in monthly data in value terms are the higher commodity prices that prevailed a year ago and increases in the value of the US dollar compared with most other currencies.

Source: WTO (2009c, p. 2 and p. 18)

One relatively easy and obvious point that can be cleared right away is that two 'WTO explanations' for the strength and speed of the trade collapse relate to the monetary value of trade flows. Monetary variations are of course relevant for the interpretation of the headline figures on international trade which are often in current prices and US dollars, but these measurement issues do not have an impact on changes in trade volume which is what we will study in this book.[3]

It is true that price movements played an important role in the 1930s due to the occurrence of a process of deflation which worsened the depression, but this was not the case in 2008–2009 (see Figure 1.4 below).[4] Anyhow, since we will be studying the changes in trade *volumes* we will have to look for other reasons for the world trade collapse.[5]

In any case it is noteworthy that many of the proposed explanations for the 2008–2009 trade collapse have not been put to the test yet, essentially because data are not available (a) for a sufficiently long period or (b) at the level of detail that is necessary to test some of the 'explanations' – which actually are still 'hypotheses' and should be treated accordingly. This book will discuss and investigate these hypotheses and where appropriate and possible will attempt to provide tests of their validity. As will become clear it is not easy to find the 'smoking gun' as indeed other researchers (for example Levchenko et al. 2009) have also pointed out.

A Complete Surprise

It is, moreover, a truism that the trade collapse took the economic profession completely by surprise.[6] Between December 2007 when the financial crisis started and July 2009, the OECD, for example, revised its prediction for the growth rate of world trade from +8 per cent to –16 per cent, that is an unprecedented 24 percentage points revision (see Figure 1.2).[7] Importantly, other international organizations such as the World Bank, the WTO and IMF did no better. During 2009 global trade projections were continuously revised downward. By the beginning of July 2009 they revised their April 2009 projections (World Bank 2009a; WTO 2009a and IMF 2009a) of –6.1 per cent, –9 per cent and –11 per cent, respectively to –9.7 per cent, –10 per cent, and –12.2 per cent, respectively (World Bank 2009b, WTO 2009b and IMF 2009b). A protracted recession scenario drawn up by the World Bank in the summer of 2009 (World Bank 2009b, p. 33) included shrinkage of –11.9 per cent in 2009 and, additionally, –4.7 per cent in 2010.[8]

Indeed, it is unfortunate but true that this crisis shows again that the economic profession is a lot better in explaining *post mortem* why the patient died than in predicting the advent of the deglobalization virus (or its defeat, for that matter).

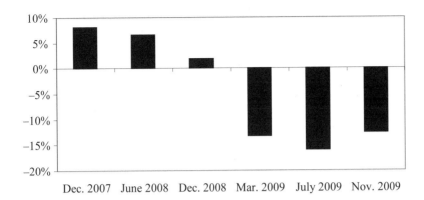

Dec. 2007   June 2008   Dec. 2008   Mar. 2009   July 2009   Nov. 2009

Sources: OECD (2007, 2008a,b and 2009a,b,c)

*Figure 1.2   How the OECD changed its predictions for world trade in the
            year 2009*

Neglecting the Black Swan

A key question for empirical researchers is of course whether anything can be
said at all. It may be the case that structural change presently is so far-
reaching that econometric analysis (based as it is on past experiences) cannot
be used to analyse and/or predict the impact of key economic events. This is
especially true for the significant changes in economic relationships and
policies (including the sudden revival of old-fashioned but appropriate
Keynesian demand stabilization) as witnessed in 2008 and 2009.

Admittedly, it has been possible in the past to estimate meaningful
econometric models that continued to work during significant changes in
international regimes (examples are van Bergeijk and Oldersma 1990
regarding the fall of the Iron Curtain and van Bergeijk and Berk 2001
regarding the creation of monetary union in Europe). So econometric analysis
per se is not inappropriate, even regarding seemingly unique events such as
the world trade collapse. The point, however, is that much of the recent work
that has been done on post Second World War data simply is inappropriate
for the analysis of the present crisis because it does not include the Black
Swan of the 1930s (cf. Taleb 2007).[9] A Black Swan is a large-impact, low-
probability event. Due to their infrequent occurrence such events are
obviously difficult if not impossible to predict.[10] Often Black Swans are
treated by econometricians as outliers or such events are simply ignored. Of
course the data for the interbellum appear to be less comprehensive and more

inaccurate, but that is no reason to neglect the 1930s. This is especially the case because we have so few observations on world trade collapses.

Actually, the problem is that many economists often appear to behave in the manner of the proverbial drunk who prefers to look for his lost key under the street light and not in the alley (where it was lost) because it is dark over there. Indeed, when economists embark on the road of a specific methodology they will often restrict their analysis to country groupings and periods for which the required data are available. In practice this means that the available analyses often deal with the experiences of a subset of OECD countries after the Second World War period. Many country studies deal with the US only or use US data as a proxy for global conditions (examples are Cheung and Guichard 2009 and Levchenko et al. 2009). Although these studies may be informative, there is no indication (or logic) that the findings for the US can be generalized to other countries or to the global level. The focus on readily available data is not only a waste of available but imperfect observations that cover longer periods; it also implies that the observation that really matters (that is the trade collapse of the 1930s) is not a part of the analysis.

One contribution of this book is that I will not go for the perfect data or method, but that I am prepared to distil sensible evidence from whatever data available, exercising judgement in the interpretation of this evidence. (One exception to this rule should be mentioned right away and that is that China has not been included in the analysis because the data collection and reporting in my opinion are not trustworthy and comparable to other countries.) The methodology is sensible since clearly longer periods and broader country coverage are needed so as to include more cases of the infrequent phenomenon of world trade collapse.

1. A UNIQUE PHENOMENON?

Indeed, declines in the volume of world trade do not occur very often. Defining 'trade recessions' as situations in which trade decreases for two months in a row, Faber and van Marrewijk (2009) have analysed the two most recent decades of monthly world trade data.[11] Faber and van Marrewijk find only two other world trade recessions: the Asian Crisis (when their indicator decreased from June 1998 to August 1998, inclusive) and the Dotcom Crisis (where the trade recession is dated as January–October 2001). Using a slightly less restrictive definition and focussing on OECD trade rather than on global trade, Araújo and Oliveira Martins (2009) study trade data that cover the period 1965–2007. They find only six periods of negative OECD trade (their worst case is 1982 when OECD trade contracted by about 14 per cent). It is worth pointing out that the level of aggregation matters for the frequency with which periods of negative real trade growth are being established. Araújo and Oliveira Martins (2009), for example, report that months of negative trade growth below 10 per cent occur in 2.4 per cent of the research period for total OECD trade, but in 4.3 to 6.5 per cent of the research period for the individual country data of France, Germany, Italy, Japan, the UK and the US. Negative trade growth is of course even more unlikely to occur on an annual basis, but when we increase the research period and also include the 1930s, then the phenomenon would seem to be less infrequent that suggested by those analyses that focus on the recent period only.

Using annual trade data for the period 1880–2009, Figure 1.3 illustrates the occurrence of negative annual growth rates for world trade: 12 per cent of the real annual growth rates are negative. Decreases in the volume of *world* trade are thus relatively unique in recent history, but they do occur. It is, however, not only the fact that negative world trade growth occurs with a very low frequency which makes the 2009 world trade collapse an intriguing phenomenon. Also the strength of the decrease is remarkable. The starkest declines in the figure are 1932 and 2009 (note that the 2009 figure is a preliminary estimate).[12] (Chapter 2 takes a more detailed look at the individual country experiences over this period.)

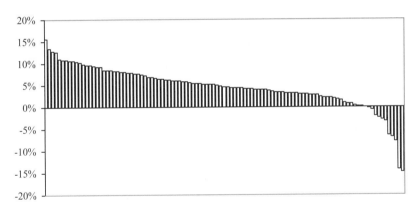

Sources: Calculations based on real trade data for 1880–1991 from Maddison (1995) and for 1992–2009 from *CPB World Trade Monitor*

Figure 1.3   Real annual growth rates in per cent for world trade sorted in decreasing order (1880–2009)

On the Brink of Deglobalization

Two World Trade Collapses Compared

A decrease in the volume of world trade of this magnitude has actually not occurred in the post Second World War era. We have to go back to the Great Depression and its aftermath to see a comparable destruction of world trade. Figure 1.4 by way of illustration compares the time path of the trade collapse in the 1930s to that of the trade crunch that started in October 2008, showing the developments of both values and volumes of world trade. Setting the peak at time 0, we can see how trade values and trade volumes continuously increased in the eight years prior to the outburst of both crises and decreased in the years after the peak (the lines in the graph that describe the recent trade collapse have been identified with square markers). In general the real world trade numbers during the two trade collapses so far follow more or less the same pattern, but as the 2008 trade collapse (possibly) moves into its third year it is still too early to tell whether the world economy will follow a comparable trajectory or whether a quicker rebound will occur. The nominal data show clear differences both in the running up to the crisis and in the development during the trade collapses: in contrast to the 1930s when price movements played an important role, values and volumes during the most recent trade collapse appear to have been moving more or less in tandem.

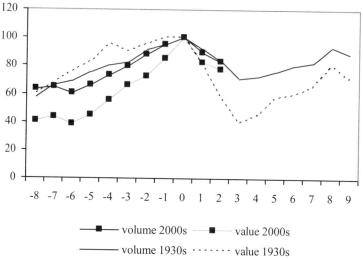

Notes: End of period observations with the exception of 2009. Peak year is 0

Sources: UN Statistical Office (1962), Table I and calculations based on CPB trade monitor

Figure 1.4 Real and nominal world trade before and during the two world trade collapses (index numbers; peak year = 100)

Figure 1.4 thus contradicts the nominal explanations put forward by the WTO in its *World Trade Report 2009* for the strength and speed of the trade collapse. This can be compared to findings by Levchenko et al. (2009, p. 6) who conclude from a detailed sector analysis of US statistics that

it is remarkable that in some important sectors, such as automotive, capital goods, and consumer goods, the prices did not move at all, and the entire decline in nominal exports and exports is accounted for by real quantities.

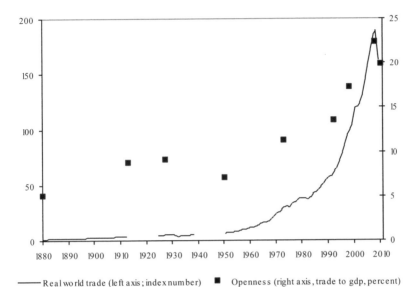

———— Real world trade (left axis; index number)　■　Openness (right axis, trade to gdp, percent)

Sources:　Real trade data 1880–1992 and trade to GDP ratios 1880–1998: Maddison (1995) and (2001). Real trade data 1992–2009QI *CPB World Trade Monitor.* Trade-to-GDP ratios 2008 and 2010 constructed on the basis of IMF World Economic Outlook Database, April 2009, and have been updated in the basis of IMF (2009b)

Figure 1.5 Historical perspectives on the 2009 trade collapse

It is even possible to put these developments into a longer and more comprehensive historical perspective. Figure 1.5 summarizes data for the development of real world trade since 1880. The line in the graph relates to the left axis and presents index numbers with 1998 as a base year. Since the end of the 19th century world trade had steadily been growing with the exception of the interbellum when a strong break occurred in the long-term trend and the global trade curve shifted downwards. Since the Second World War world trade increased 25-fold and from this perspective the first oil shock in 1973 and the stagflation of the 1980s show up as mere ripples. So the six decades before 2009 constituted an exceptional chapter in the history of world trade indeed.

Equally exceptional are both the speed and the depth of the downturn of the 2008 trade collapse. Eichengreen and O'Rourke (2009) estimate that the trade collapse in the first year of the 2008–2009 trade collapse was about double the decline that occurred in the similar phase of the Great Depression. Araúlo and Oliveira-Martins (2009), moreover, see the exceptionally synchronized character of the downturn as a key characteristic: at the end of 2008 more than 90 per cent of the OECD countries suddenly and simultaneously experienced a decline of their individual trade flows in excess of 10 per cent.

More importantly, it is not only the volume of trade which drifts away from its long-term trend; also openness (that is trade in relation to production) is showing a steep and unique decline (see Estevadeordal et al. 2003 for an historic interpretation of this ratio). The square markers in Figure 1.5 relate to the right axis and summarize a well-known measure of openness, namely the trade-to-GDP ratio (in per cent).[13] The development of openness again illustrates both the unprecedented impact of the Great Depression and the extraordinarily developments in 2009. Based on recent IMF projections, the world appears to be experiencing its most significant decrease in openness since the 1930s.

Similarities

But are the 1930s a look-alike of the 2000s? Interestingly, many contemporary observations in the interbellum suggest so. Although one could resort to many contemporary observers, I select a clear example of a very rational observer that was intellectually occupied with many of the issues that are central to the present book.[14] Two years ago I discovered in an obscure second-hand bookshop in The Hague a booklet on the business cycle, the economic outlook and the still uncertain impact of what is nowadays known as the Great Depression that was written by the Dutch Noble Price laureate Jan Tinbergen in 1933 (Tinbergen, 1933). Tinbergen's description of his world (incidentally, much like many studies of his contemporaries) shows remarkable similarities with how we ourselves would today describe the globalizing economy at the start of the third millennium (compare Table 1.1).

- Life expectancy increased in the early twentieth century as happened in the greying societies at the end of that epoch.
- Tinbergen noted a strong international reallocation of production towards the periphery ('primitive countries that only recently have become capitalist') in the same manner that many observe today would

describe how the collapse of communism has stimulated the entry of China and other previously centrally planned economies into the world economic system.

- Communication (intercontinental and wireless telegraph) and transport (at the end of the era of sailing and the start of commercial air flight) improved and he studied the important consequences of these innovations: cost reductions and the fact that 'mental horizons' shrunk so that new far-away markets were becoming realistic opportunities. In technical economic terms the extent of potential markets increased significantly. Likewise, modern generations witnessed the advent of the container and the Internet, the former being a major transportation cost-reducing innovation, the latter being an equally important cost-reducing factor for the dissemination of knowledge and ideas.
- New products came on the market, such as cars and radios. Likewise the introduction of (portable) computers and mobile phones implied tremendous opportunities both for hardware providers and for producers of content.
- These new industries according to Tinbergen boosted the economy and fuelled the stock exchange booms − not only on their own account but also because they were helped tremendously by financial innovations such as consumer credit and the emergence of investment trust. It goes without saying that financial innovation was also characteristic of the 2000s.
- If anything unrealistic optimism dominated the period before the two trade collapses.

Table 1.1 Some differences and similarities of the context of the 1930s and the 2008 trade collapse

	1930s	2000s
Long-run reductions of trade costs	●	●
New modes of transportation and communication	●	●
Entry of new countries (recent capitalist countries)	●	●
Key innovations	●	●
Financial innovation	●	●
Worldwide crisis	●	●
Trade collapse most pronounced in manufacturing	●	●
Price decreases as an important driver of the trade collapse	●	
Trade mainly based on comparative advantage	●	
Substantial presence of international value chains		●

All in all the 1930s and the 2000s share a lot of characteristics, in particular perhaps regarding the optimistic view on the future of the economy. Innovations and internationalization were seen as strong trends that were expected to dominate the outlook for the world economy.

Differences

On the other hand (and particularly regarding the characteristics of the international trade flows) important differences should be noted between the two periods. Trade in the interbellum was much more in conformity with the neoclassical model of comparative advantage in which countries specialize in different products, whereas intra-industry trade (in which a country may export and import the same manner of products) is an increasingly important characteristic of modern international trade. This is true even in a North–South and South–South context. Much trade is intra-company trade that takes place within multinational corporations that manage international value chains taking advantage of location advantages around the globe. So similarity and differences abound.

It may at first glance seem to be a bit disappointing that no clear-cut case of trade collapse exists, but it is important that some variation exists because that helps us to formulate and test hypotheses. Formulating and testing theories after all is the royal road to a better understanding of this phenomenon. It is also important that we have more than one case because that really opens the door to economic analysis. The historian Rothermund (1996, p. 1), for example, claims (about the analysis of the Great Depression):

> It seems that this was a unique event and such events can only be explained historically as they defy the laws of economics.[15]

While one would perhaps not completely want to agree with the logic of this argument, many would say that Rothermund definitely had a point ... but of course only until the second world trade collapse in 2008.

2. IS THIS A FOURTH PHASE IN MODERN WORLD TRADE HISTORY?

Let us now turn to the question of whether a new phase of de-globalization is a likely scenario. Figure 1.5 rather dramatically illustrated the second reversal of the globalization process. This is a message, however, that needs to be brought with a bit more nuance as the same figure also clarifies that the world is still much more open today than it ever was in the previous century.

Moreover, due to the exceptionally long period of strong growth the human eye observes an exaggerated development in the volume of trade for more recent years. A better way to represent this manner of data is to use a logarithmic transformation of the observations as is done for the same period and data in Figure 1.6. We can now see better that the reduction of the trade volume in the interbellum was stronger (in per cent) than the recent developments (but note again that we still do not know for certain if the trade collapse will continue or that trade by the end of 2009 had hit a sustainable bottom). Since Figure 1.6 uses a logarithmic scale, exponential growth of world trade is represented by a straight line: different slopes in the graph represent different rates of growth.

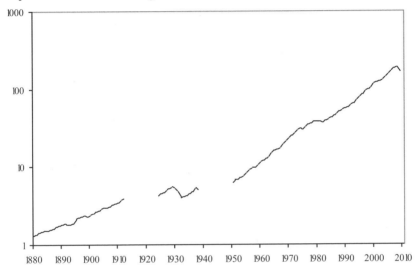

Sources: See Figure 1.5

Figure 1.6 World trade volume 1880–2009 (logarithmic scale)

We can thus readily observe three phases in the development of real world trade. Since the end of the 19th century world trade has steadily grown with the exception of the interbellum when a strong break occurred in the long-term trend and the global trade curve shifted downwards. Between 1880 and the First World War a real annual growth rate of about 3.5 per cent was registered and world trade increased twenty-fold. In the post Second World War period real growth was significantly stronger at 5.5 per cent per annum. Figure 1.6 thus illustrates the well-known economic historical narrative of the rise and fall of world trade since the industrial revolution, which according to Estevadeordal et al. (2003, pp. 368–70) is based on a consensus view. This consensus sees the drive to the modern levels of internationalization as a consequence of the spreading of the free trade doctrine, giving rise to an 'age' of liberal economic policies and technological innovations that led to a strong decline in trade costs. This narrative sees the onset of trade stagnation after the First World War as a consequence of bad economic policies, in particular the continued adherence to the Gold Standard in the wake of the Great Depression which forced the 'Gold countries' to apply protectionist trade policies including higher tariffs, more quotas and other distorting commercial policies. The restoration of globalization would take from the end of the Second World War to the 1970s when the internationalization of production became again comparable to the levels at the start of the twentieth century.[16]

The consensus view sees income growth as one of the drivers of the second wave of the growth of trade in the most recent phase of globalization. This view that income growth drives world trade has been very influential. It has given rise to the idea of a multiplier that magnifies fluctuations in income. This multiplier (also known as the elasticity of world trade to world income) has reportedly increased since the 1960s (see, for example, Freund 2009a) and this empirical finding is often explained with reference to the international fragmentation of production and the growth of international value chains. In addition there is also some evidence for a second structural break around 1990, but this is less convincing (at least the alternative hypothesis of 'no break' cannot be rejected; see Cheung and Guichard 2009, p. 13). We will return to some of these issues in Chapter 4.

Trade Frictions

Recent scientific research on the trade collapse and the actual experiences before and during the years 2007–2009 have uncovered some nasty challenges for the traditional explanation of the booms and busts of world trade over the last two centuries pointing out that trade was stimulated (hindered) by decreases (increases) of certain friction parameters. A useful classification of trade frictions is developed by Estevadeordal et al. (2003). They distinguish three types of trade frictions:

- *Payment frictions*, related to the international exchange system and uncertainties regarding the future value of currencies and the possibilities to make international payments in an efficient way.
- *Policy frictions*, related to trade policies (tariffs, quota, etc., but also multilateral and bilateral agreements) and commercial policies (including export subsidies).
- *Transport frictions*, mainly related to transportation and communication costs.

Estevadeordal et al. (2003) econometrically identify drivers of the world trade collapse in the 1930s that differ from the consensus view. A first finding is the observation that the breakdown of the Gold Standard implied a collapse of the international payment system which brings in a relevant factor in the analysis – the so-called payment friction – that of course can also be recognized in the shock to trust and confidence in banks during the 2000s. Also and importantly, protectionism does not appear to have functioned as a trigger for the world trade collapse.[17] Both in the interbellum and in the recent trade collapse the volume of world trade was already declining when protectionism still stood at historically low levels. So policy frictions appear to have been less important (if at all) in the first phase of the two trade collapses. Finally, the perceived reductions in distance frictions (often equated to transportation costs) may not have been the driver behind the development of world trade. Payment frictions will be addressed in Chapter 3 and policy frictions in Chapter 5, but it pays to consider the issue of transport frictions in more detail now.

The transport friction
In the roaring 1920s the advent of wireless radio, commercial air flight and other innovations were assumed to reduce the distance between countries and thus to increase trade amongst them. Likewise, around the turn of the millennium it was increasingly being argued that globalization reduced the distance between countries due to the Internet, lower transportation costs and the ease of travelling and communication. The death of distance was announced by amongst others Cairncross (1997) and Friedman (2005). Their hypotheses gained ground in the popular press and amongst policy makers: a truly 'global village' had emerged in which the difference between external (international) trade and internal (domestic) trade no longer seemed to be relevant: the world – in the words of Friedman – had become 'flat'.

But had it? Essentially, this is an empirical question and a topic of much debate among trade economists. A counterintuitive finding of the empirical literature is that the impact of distance, despite stronger globalization, has at least remained as important as it used to be for the geography of international trade. An example is provided by the meta-analysis of the scientific literature by Disdier and Head (2008). They report on the basis of 103 scientific econometric studies for the years 1870–2000 and a good 1500 estimated distance parameters. Their analysis shows that the distance decay effect is on average one third stronger in the more recent period 1990–2000 compared to the average finding for the years 1870–1970. This result is a general finding in the modern empirical trade literature.[18] It is an illustration of the fact that distance frictions are not always on a downward trend especially over the period 1950–2000, although the results reported by different authors for more recent years are not completely consistent and seem to be mainly driven by reductions in border taxes. Interestingly, broadly defined trade costs appear to have increased in the run up to both trade collapses (see, for example, Estevadeordal et al. 2003 on the 1930s and Jacks et al. 2009 and Campbell et al. 2009 on the recent world trade collapse). Moreover, the causality with regard to trade frictions is not unproblematic: reductions in trade costs may be the drivers of world trade, but transportation costs may also decrease endogenously due to increasing volumes of trade. Indeed, to complicate matters even more: geographical trends in transportation costs are contradictory as decreases for the maritime transport costs for trade originating in Europe and Northern America contrast with increases for harbours located in Japan, Australia and New Zealand and this may reflect buoyant trade from Asia. If so transportation costs responded endogenously to changes in the geographical pattern of trade (see Boulhol and de Serres, 2010) and possibly may also have done so to the overall volume of trade.

Knowledge is Preliminary

Other issues about which we can only speculate are whether the world economic system hit a sustainable bottom in 2009, how long the apparent period of deglobalization could last and what the drivers of these processes will be. Such issues may actually remain on the table for quite some time as was the case during the 1930s when even the most educated and rational analysts found it difficult to gauge whether the crisis was permanent or temporary. An example is Jan Tinbergen who in 1933 (so four years into the Great Depression) wisely admitted that he did not know the answer and concluded that the question about the duration of the crisis could not be predicted with any confidence by economic science.[19] Moreover, also in the years before 2007 quite a few empirical studies were published that contested the findings of earlier analyses of the 1930s. If a scientific consensus can still be attacked (and possibly change) after so long a period we should be prepared to keep an open mind, especially during the first decade after the start of the recent world trade collapse. Given the preliminary state of our knowledge any result should thus be treated with caution.

3. IN NEED OF A NEW NARRATIVE

The key message of this book is that the narrative that, so to say, developed on the wave of the world trade collapse is not to be trusted and actually is contradicted by many observations. The profession was perhaps too eager to provide *the* story that explained everything and trade analysts forgot to check the facts. Wrong-footed economists were actually not helped by the coincidence that the necessary data to test their theories were not available because statistical series had recently been discontinued (as in the case of trade finance), simply did not exist or were under construction (as in the case of the extent of vertical specialization in trade). Another handicap of the profession was its recent focus on the microeconomics of heterogeneous firms which not only led to a neglect of well-established macroeconomic relationships, but also may have exposed the analysis to two separate but related problems that always have been a particular nuisance in economics: the micro–macro paradox and the fallacy of composition.[20]

The micro–macro paradox occurs when the empirical analysis of micro data apparently does not support the results that are based on macro data. An example is the finding that firms do not become more productive while they internationalize their commercial activities. This contrasts with the fact that the macroeconomic welfare increase of internationalization (openness) is well established. This micro–macro paradox of international economics can be reconciled when we consider, for example, the effects of industry restructuring, that is the Schumpeterian process by which more productive firms drive out less productive firms.[21] The implication is that a robust analysis often requires the simultaneous analysis of micro and macro data.

The fallacy of composition is a logical problem that can occur if one deduces from findings at the microeconomic level (that is at the level of firms, consumers or industries) what is happening at the macroeconomic level (that is at the level of the national or world economy), but neglects the interactions between individuals or sectors. An example is the sales contraction in international value chains. One explanation for this phenomenon is that value chains are important forward and backward transmitters of a demand shock and thus cause a fall in sales along the full chain (and thereby of international trade). An alternative explanation, however, is a process of substitution away from value chain activities so that international sales in the value chain contract while other international sales increase. The first explanation implies an unambiguous decrease in international trade. The alternative explanation (the contraction of trade in the value chain would be consequence rather than cause) may ceteris paribus increase international trade (or lead to a smaller contraction).

Anyhow, it is noteworthy that the factors that were the usual suspects during the first phase of the trade collapse – the fragmentation of production in international value chains, protectionism and trade finance – appear with hindsight to have been merely innocent bystanders. There is actually some evidence that one of these bystanders (the international business to business networks) may even have done a lot of good for the global economy in times of crisis. This book hopes to contribute to a new narrative of the recent crisis (and may at the same time provide a fresh perspective on the potential causes of the trade collapse in the 1930s).

The need for a new narrative does not only reflect the need for intellectual honesty and clarity. Policy advice based on misperceived causes will be harmful. It prevents finding the right answers to the present crisis and to the trade collapses that undoubtedly will hit the world economy in the future. The risk of the verdict of the first phase thus is that these errors continue to be echoed in policy advice and economic analyses around the world. Keynes ([1936] 1986, p. 383) already noted that

> The ideas of economists and political philosophers, both when they are right and when they are wrong, are more powerful than is commonly understood. Indeed the world is ruled by little else. Practical men, who believe themselves to be quite exempt from any intellectual influence, are usually the slaves of some defunct economist. Madmen in authority, who hear voices in the air, are distilling their frenzy from some academic scribbler of a few years back.

4. PLAN OF THE BOOK

The next chapter starts with an empirical description of the experiences of some 45–50 countries during three periods: the 1930s, 1980–2006 and the recent period of trade collapse from 2007 to 2010. It provides a discussion of measurement issues and an argumentation to analyse *import* developments. The empirical part of the chapter analyses how 18 major post-1980 financial crises have impacted on import volumes of individual countries. Next detailed analyses of import developments at the level of individual countries are provided for the two ultimate cases of world trade collapse. One of the important stylized facts is that individual country experiences differ a lot. This is true for the relatively homogeneous set of OECD countries in the years following 2007 and applies *a fortiori* for the other periods and other countries and country groupings that are investigated. The key research implication that follows from this observation and that makes up the body of the next chapters is the importance of understanding why these country experiences diverge.

Chapter 3 deals with the two major international capital flows that have an impact on international trade: foreign direct investment (FDI) and trade finance. One key theme explored in this chapter is substitution. Often a consequence of increasing FDI is that trade flows are reduced because export to a country is substituted so to say by building up production facilities for that product in that country. The strong reduction in FDI which is a reflection of investment plans being postponed and/or even put off may actually have supported the volume of world trade to some extent because some international trade opportunities have not been cannibalized by the international reallocation of production facilities. Countervailing forces may also have been at work in formal and informal financial markets. In many discussions of the world trade collapse trade finance and trade credit are seen as more or less the same, but as we will see they are actually substitutes during a financial crisis that move in opposite directions: when banks reduce or withdraw credit, final arrangements like vendor or buyer credit become more important. Chapter 3 also reviews the available empirical literature pointing out many inconsistencies (and thus suggesting new issues for future research), but the final conclusion is that it is unlikely that a trade finance squeeze sparked the world trade collapse.

Chapter 4 describes and discusses international value chains and some measurement issues that may explain the simultaneous upward trends in globalization (measured by the trade-to-GDP ratio) and the share of value chain activity in total trade. The available empirical evidence on the relationship between, on the one hand, the strength of the decline and/or the speed of transmission in international value chains and, on the other hand, the relationship between shares of manufacturing trade, intra-industry trade and vertical specialization is inconclusive. The evidence suggests that international value chains have *not* been an important driver behind the trade collapse (as has been assumed by many authors). International value chains actually may have cushioned trade reductions.

Chapter 5 focuses on yet another factor (protectionism) that has unjustifiably been on the shortlist of potential drivers of the trade collapse. The chapter discusses (the political economy of) protectionism, describes recent patterns of protectionism and clarifies that protectionism cannot explain the 2008–2009 trade collapse (neither has it been the factor that set the trade collapse in the 1930s in motion). In addition the chapter sketches three scenarios for the future development of protectionism.

Following three chapters in which potential explanations are taken from the long list, Chapter 6 adds a potential driver of the trade collapse, as it develops and applies an alternative: the theory of trade uncertainty. An important theoretical finding is the existence of an information and/or co-ordination externality in decentralized market economies that induces too strong an international specialization pattern in such economies. Alternative theories that may yield similar relationships between specialization and political structures will be discussed and the chapter also reflects on observed patterns of political responses to trade disruption.

Chapter 7 provides an empirical analysis of one of the building blocks of the standard narrative of the world trade collapse, that is the value chain hypothesis, and tests this against the trade uncertainty hypothesis. A cross-section analysis of the depth and duration of import decline in 45 countries and over 2007–2009Q3 shows that the presence of value chains has not increased the trade collapse at the level of individual countries. The econometric analysis confirms one of the predictions of the theory of trade uncertainty namely the weaker decline and the longer duration of the import adjustment in decentralized economies.

Chapter 8 sketches some economic and political second order effects of the process of deglobalization. The final chapter also takes up the issue of trade policy. It discusses the idea that trade barriers and import substitution are often seen as solutions in times of depression and illustrates that the current crisis is not different in this respect. The empirical evidence presented in this book, however, will show the risks of policies that digress in this direction. Since a shock increase in trade uncertainty must have been one of the key determinants of the world trade collapse it is the reduction of this uncertainty that is the first best policy recipe.

NOTES

[1] Two useful collections of state of the art assessments are: Baldwin and Evenett (2009) and Evenett et al. (2009).

[2] The *World Trade Report 2009* does not repeat one of the explanations mentioned by its director-general during his pre-April G20 press conference (WTO 2009b) namely that ' production for many products is sourced around the world so there is a multiplier effect – as demand falls sharply overall, trade will fall even further'. Disappointingly, the World Trade Report published a full quarter later only rephrased this press note.

[3] Note, however, that exchange rate variability increases trade uncertainty and this may deter international specialization.

[4] See Berthou and Emlinger (2009) for a detailed analysis of price and quantity movements. They find substantial shifts in the share of products differentiated by quality levels. In their analyses the reduction in demand for high-quality–high-price goods explains about two percentage points of the world trade collapse.

[5] Price movements and currency fluctuations imply of course relevant *measurement* issues especially for the price indices that are used to deflate the import values. It is, however, too early to know if and in which direction this distorts the reported quantity indices.

[6] A notable exception is Lehman (2008).

[7] The OECD world trade model is discussed in some detail in Chapter 3, section 3. The model is described and analyzed in Cheung and Guichard (2009).

[8] The international organizations, however, continued to agree in the sense that they foresaw that trade would hit bottom soon and that positive growth would return on average in 2010.

9   This point goes beyond the so-called 'Lucas Critique' (Lucas 1976) that policy regime shifts change the structure of the economic system under investigation because quantitative changes of policy instruments will influence the coefficients of the estimated behavioural equations, as the expectations of firms and households (as well as the restrictions under which economic subjects maximize) depend on parameters indirectly related to the considered policy instruments. A critical discussion on the generality and applicability of the Lucas critique is van Bergeijk (1999) and van Bergeijk and Berk (2001).

10   It should be noted, however, that general collapses and crises (rather than trade collapses) occur in the international system with much higher frequency probably because of the inherent instabilities that increase when systems become more complex and integrated. It is almost a law in economics that economic subjects neglect or confuse the signals that critical forces are building up or that something really bad has happened. A very good account of the psychological mechanisms (disaster myopia and cognitive dissonance) that drive this collective human ostrich behaviour is Guttentag and Herring (1986).

11   Faber and van Marrewijk (2009) use a five months centred average. Note that if this indicator turns negative for two consecutive months, the volume of trade will have contracted for two quarters which is in line with the usual definition of an economic recession (namely two quarters of negative GDP growth).

12   Other years with strong negative annual growth rates are 1939, 1931 and 1938.

13   Admittedly, this is a crude measure for globalization of international trade as it does not consider the network and interconnectedness of the world trade system, but this is the only measure available for this long time span (cf. Arribas et al 2008).

14   One such contemporary observer would be Keynes ([1919] 1984, pp. 6–7).

15   Rothermund is just a recent example of how historians see the great depression. See also Kindleberger (1978, pp. 14–15 and 21–2) on this topic.

16   Serrano (2007), for example, dates the 'phase transition' in the globalization of trade in the 1960s, suggesting the emergence of a new kind of relationship between world trade and world production around the start of the 1960s.

17   An alternative interpretation is that the measurement of the restrictiveness of trade policies is not measured accurately. See, for example, Anderson and Neary (2005).

18   See, for example, Linders (2006) and van Bergeijk (2009a). However, Brun et al. (2005) report a reduced impact of distance.

19   'Uit het voorgaande blijkt wel dat de vraag over de duur van deze krisis en depressie door de wetenschap niet met een grote zekerheid kan worden voorspeld' (Tinbergen 1933, p. 177).

20   And of course the fallacy of hasty generalization may have played havoc on the early attempts to say something about the drivers of the world trade collapse.

21   See van Bergeijk (2009a, Chapter 4).

Appendix 1A.1: Notes on Measuring (De)Globalization

This appendix discusses some measurement issues related to trade and trade openness in the context of historical and/or cross-country comparisons (the appendix is partially based on van Bergeijk and Mensink 1997). Obviously, this is an important topic for this book both because I compare the 1930s and the 2008–2009 period and because I analyse the different country experiences. Section 1 deals with measurement errors in international statistics, in particular import, export and foreign direct investment. Section 2 deals with trade openness – which is the ratio of trade to gross domestic product – and, consequently, also deals with international income comparisons. Readers not interested in measurement issues are urged to read this appendix.

1. MEASUREMENT OF TRADE AND INVESTMENT

Oskar Morgenstern's well-known 1950 study *On the Accuracy of Economic Observations* uncovered that accepted economic figures often have very large error components. Morgenstern (1950, pp. 137–80) investigated foreign trade statistics in detail concluding that a measurement error of 25 per cent in trade statistics actually is a 'good result'. Even with respect to international gold movements between Central Banks (a trade which by the nature of both the product and the administrator should be registered close to perfect), Morgenstern discovered measurement errors of 50 per cent.

So a first step of measuring any phenomenon related to international flows is to consider *ex ante* what could be the optimal estimation method on the basis of an error prognosis. In the case of (de)globalization two aspects need examination: the error rates of the variables concerned and the registration method of international merchandise trade. Different error rates characterize the variables that could be used in the investigation, such as exports, imports, trade, foreign direct investments, lending and other financial flows. Exports and imports can be aggregated into total trade and can be disaggregated by commodity or by trade partner, and this may also influence the error rate. In principle the best or most reliable estimate will result when the variable with the lowest error rate is used. The impact of the registration system of trade and investment statistics needs careful examination as well. For example we may not want measurement to be influenced by the fact that costs and tariffs have fluctuated substantially during the period under discussion.

Note, however, that the exactness and distinctness of the measurement procedure *per se* is not a goal on itself. Often research requires that a trade-off is made between data availability, conceptual relevance and measurement and this is not different for this book.

Error Rates of Trade and Investment

Two determinants of error rates need to be addressed: which variable is measured most accurately, and the appropriate level of aggregation. International trade is an economic variable for which long and – and comparatively speaking – reliable time series are available. Tariffs on exports and imports used to be an important source of government receipts, and policy-makers have always had a strategic interest in the balance of trade. Hence, the trade registration system is quite well developed and details on the commodity composition of trade and the global network of bilateral trade relations are well covered (allowing *inter alia* for consistency checks). In contrast, foreign direct investment is a 'less visible' item on the balance of payments. Investment is not a well-developed base for taxation. (Actually taxation may deflect such flows.) Differences in procedures, periodicity, and (dis)aggregation (either by type or by country) have for a long time created an atmosphere of pessimism about the comparability and reliability of foreign direct investment data (see, for example, Vukmanic et al. 1985) and although the registration system has improved in recent decades due to endeavours by UNCTAD, many problems still remain. A good overview of the problems that plague statistics on Foreign Direct Investment is the UN Economic and Social Council (2008). It is worth quoting the conclusion in full

> The conclusion is that, notwithstanding all the recent efforts to make improvements, there is every reason to continue interpreting FDI data with a critical eye. For the fog has not yet fully lifted. However, more intensive cooperation, the exchange of data, including micro data, can help to improve the quality of FDI statistics and make these a still more useful tool (UN Economic and Social Council 2008, p. 2).

Indeed, a lot of scope exists for further improvement. Anyhow, for historic data the problems are widely acknowledged. Especially if one wants to analyse longer periods that also include the twentieth century one will encounter these problems. Time series are often discontinued, and changes and differences in definition hamper a proper interpretation in a historical long-term context. The availability of data is problematic from the point of view of filling the global matrix of inward and outward bilateral trade flows. Even within the OECD full country coverage is of a relatively recent data: in 1950 only five countries reported these data to the OECD; it took until the mid-1980s to get all OECD countries reporting.

Van Bergeijk (1995) investigates the minimal measurement errors that are consistent with generally accepted figures on international transactions supplied by the national statistical offices to the IMF and the OECD. Using the German and Dutch registration of their bilateral monthly trade flows (exports and imports) in the period 1977–1990, van Bergeijk reports that measurement errors in trade are at least 1.5 to 3 per cent (note that Germany and Holland are adjacent countries so that the difference can by definition not be due to transportation costs or (de)stocking). In addition the remarkable stability of the Deutsche Mark–Gulden exchange rate over this period excludes exchange rate fluctuations as a potential source of registration error. So the difference must be caused by genuine measurement error. The accuracy of foreign direct investment data is even less: using data for 20 OECD countries in the years 1950–1989 van Bergeijk finds minimal measurement errors of at least 6 per cent for the level of outward foreign direct investment and at least 14 per cent for inward foreign direct investment flows. In a quarter of the cases implied minimal measurement errors are in excess of 10 per cent. Frederico and Tena (1991) have re-assessed Morgenstern's findings with respect to foreign trade prior to the Second World War. They show that using aggregate data instead of bilateral trade data may yield more reliable results, because aggregation eliminates the problem of misclassification by commodity and/or country.

Based on these considerations, the optimal method for a study of deglobalization seems to be to use trade data rather than foreign direct investment data and to do the analysis at the highest possible level of aggregation. This suggests that total trade should be analysed rather than bilateral trade or disaggregated data by commodity, a recipe that is consistently followed in this volume.

Registration

One important trend over the period under investigation is that tremendous reductions have occurred in transportation costs (although at the time the cost of transportation has increased steeply as well). So it is important to recognize that merchandise exports are registered free-on-board (f.o.b.) while merchandise imports are registered cost-insurance-freight (c.i.f.) which includes the costs of international transport, insurance and distribution.

Obviously, any historical assessment of the development of trade integration over a long time span that is based on import data, such as the import-to-GDP ratio, will be distorted by the fact that transportation costs are much higher for early periods in history. Trade integration, for example, is deflated if measured by import data, because the transportation cost component of the import value has been reduced substantially over time. Therefore if possible one should use export data in comparisons over long time periods so as to avoid this distortion. The book follows this recipe in the analysis of long-term trends, but focuses on imports in the analysis of trade collapse over the short to medium term (as discussed in Chapter 2). This is an example of a necessary trade-off between conceptual relevance and measurement accuracy.

2. THE COMPARISON OF TRADE RATIOS

Customary in measuring globalization using trade data three types of ratios can be distinguished:

- the ratio of exports to GDP,
- the ratio of imports to GDP, and
- the ratio of trade (exports and imports) to GDP.

So there are three alternatives and a trade ratio can be written as X/Y where X is exports and Y is GDP, as M/Y with M being imports, or as $(X+M)/Y$. A trade ratio has a turnover figure (traded goods at international prices; X and M) in the nominator and in the denominator a value-added figure (GDP or Y) that, in addition to internationally trade relates to non-traded goods and non-tradeables as well.

Whereas international trade is measured at international prices so that a comparison of trade figures (that is the nominator of the trade ratio) can logically be made, one should recognize that differences in the relative prices due to the existence of non-traded and non-tradeable goods hampers a proper comparison between denominators. Indeed, no easy yardstick is readily available for comparing national incomes. It is widely recognized that comparing the GDPs of countries by simply converting them at market exchange rates into a common currency unit is a very unsatisfactory method, since exchange rates usually do not reflect the relative purchasing power of the currencies. Firstly, the market exchange rate only applies to internationally traded goods and services and capital transactions. As GDP also consists of non-traded and non-tradeable goods, comparing incomes converted at market exchange rates produces misleading results. This is especially true, because services (often non-traded and non-tradeables) are relatively cheap in most developing countries. Secondly, the official exchange rate is often a poor indication of the relative scarcity of a currency when it is not freely convertible against other currencies. Finally, big fluctuations in currency values distort international comparisons if GDP is converted at market exchange rates. Therefore PPP converted GDPs should be used (see Kravis et al. 1982 and Maddison 1995). These arguments do not only apply to comparisons between economies at one point in time; they also matter for an economy that moves over time from one level of development to another. Moreover, a historical comparison of a nation's trade ratio that is based on nominal values suffers from the fact that the price increases of services exceed the price increases of manufacturers and a trade ratio at the beginning of the period of observation thus has a much smaller trade component in real terms than the same ratio at the end of that period. The upshot is that any historical comparison should be based on constant price series.

Conclusion

The best procedure to steer clear of most sources of classification error corruption would be to measure the extent of globalization using world trade (preferably using export data as this would help to prevent or reduce the possibly distortionary impact of cost reductions in transportation and distribution). A focus on world trade may also help in another way. GDP consists of consumption C, investment I and government expenditure G, net of taxes T and exports X minus imports M. Thus we can rewrite the export ratio X/Y as $X/(C+I+G-T+X-M)$ and because we are analysing the world as a whole and since one country's exports by definition are some other country's imports we may set X equal to M so that the export ratio in the global economy simplifies to $X/Y=X/(C+I+G-T)$. Now both the nominator and the denominator relate to expenditures (that is turnover figures) and the ratio can be meaningfully compared. In Chapter 1 the comparisons over time are done for world exports and world production that are expressed in constant international prices.

It should, however, be noted that while this procedure is the preferred procedure over long time horizons, problems of interpretation and quantification may be relevant for year-to-year comparisons. For example, during the crisis it was noted that the percentage fall in world GDP at current exchange rates was almost double the percentage decline of world GDP at PPP (Bénasy-Quéré et al. 2009) and that this measurement issue may thus have an impact on short-term elasticities. Note that this problem is an aggregation problem that occurs at the level of world (or regional) GDP. It is for example not relevant in Chapter 7 where import and GDP data derived from national sources for individual countries are used.

2. From Peak to Trough

In March 2009, in preparation for the April G20 meeting, the World Bank (2009a), the World Trade Organization (2009a) and the Organisation for Economic Co-operation and Development (OECD) (2009a) produced predictions for the development of world trade. The forecasts agreed that world trade in 2009 would contract although the studies disagreed on the actual rate of decrease of the volume of world trade (see Table 2.1). The predictions of the international organizations also agreed in the sense that they foresaw that world trade would hit bottom soon and that positive growth would return on average in 2010. In this sense their predictions were both dismal and optimistic at the same time. It was not clear why the predictions differed so much (estimates ranged from –6.1 to –13.2 per cent) and how the duration of trade reduction is established since the institutions had not provided detailed information about the actual models and assumptions.

Table 2.1 Predictions for world trade (April 2009, in per cent)

	2009	2010
World Bank	−6.1	2.3
WTO	−9	'recovery'
OECD	−13.2	1.5

Sources: World Bank (2009a), World Trade Organization (2009a) and OECD (2009a)

In this chapter I use an approach that provides an alternative for the modelling exercises that are typically used by the large international organizations. Recently, a number of papers have taken an historical approach focusing on the development of key economic factors in the aftermath of financial crises. Since the world trade collapses in the 1930s and 2008–2009 have been preceded by very strong financial crises, the focus on such trigger events seems to offer an appropriate research strategy for studies like the present that want to investigate 'trade recessions'. Well-known examples of papers that follow an historical approach include the studies by Laeven and Valencia (2008) and by Reinhart and Rogoff (2009). These seminal papers focus on the development during and after a financial crisis of financial and economic variables regarding the national economies that are being studied. Typically, movements in asset prices (houses and the stock market), credit, unemployment and gross domestic product are reported. Hardly any attention, however, has been paid to the development of international trade. When trade is part of the analysis, the dataset is regionally focused (Hong et al. 2009) or deals with a subset of countries such as the OECD (Claessens et al. 2008) or emerging markets (Thomas 2009). (These studies are discussed in more detail in Section 2.) Clearly, a broader perspective is in order if one wants to assess the extent and possible duration of the trade collapse that is induced by the 2007 credit crisis. This would seem to be especially relevant because, according to Thomas (2009, p. 2), 'the economic literature on the linkages between trade volumes and financing is very thin'.

This chapter attempts to fill this gap. Section 1 explains how we measure and define the beginning and end of a trade collapse and its impact. I discuss how financial crises may influence exports and imports. Section 2 argues that we should study the development of *imports* rather than of exports also because an individual financial crisis will mainly have an impact on the volume of imports (rather than exports) and discusses the available empirical evidence. Section 3 summarizes historical evidence on the impact and duration of import volume reductions in the context of individual financial crises, in particular in the post-1980/pre-2007 era. This approach is relevant in the present context because a global reduction in import demand will by definition enforce a decrease of exports for all countries. In addition Section 3 provides regional perspectives on real imports for the interbellum and the world trade collapse over the year 2007–2009. Section 4 adds individual country details for both periods of trade collapse. Section 5 draws some conclusions. In particular we will see that recent individual country experiences regarding the percentage decrease in the volume of imports differ up to a factor of three for a relatively homogeneous set of OECD countries and that it is important to understand why these country experiences diverge. The next chapters will be devoted to that question.

1. MEASURING THE TRADE COLLAPSE

In this book the standard apparatus for the analysis of business cycles is used to analyse the development of trade flows. Figure 2.1 illustrates the standard methodology and the key measurement items regarding the trade collapse. The trade cycle shows the usual cyclical pattern around an increasing trend (the dotted line). At some point in time the curve reaches its maximum (the peak) at which point the positive growth rate becomes negative. This is the start of the trade collapse. At the end of the trade collapse (the trough) the decline of the volume of trade ends and trade starts to grow again (although from a much lower level than its peak value). The period between peak and trough is called the duration of the trade collapse. Note that a positive growth rate for the volume of trade does not imply that the *status quo ante* has been restored as that would require a substantial number of positive growth rates until the previous peak level has been reached again. This period is labelled 'Recovery'. It could, however, be argued that full recovery may take even longer, namely until the trend level of world trade has been reached again (so exceeding the previous peak).[1]

Volume of trade

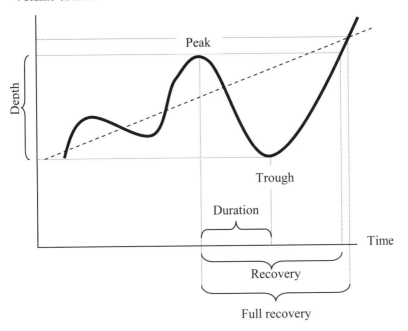

Notes: – Actual development of the volume of trade
--- Trend development of the volume of trade in the absence of the trade collapse

Figure 2.1 Peak, trough, depth, duration, recovery and full recovery

Note that early 2010 it was not yet known whether the world had reached the trough in the recent world trade collapse. At that time it was possible to identify the peak and for quite a reasonable number of countries a local minimum had been established in the trade volume series, but it was still uncertain whether positive growth rates were sustainable. It was known, however, that recovery had definitely not occurred yet and would probably take many more quarters. Actually, for a number of countries import volumes appeared to continue to decline. Figure 2.2 is based on the most recently available data at the end of 2009 for a group of 35 countries that are included in the OECD National Account Statistics database. The figure distinguishes between a group of 24 countries where the import volume was increasing again by the end of the third quarter of 2009 and a group of 11 countries where it was still decreasing (and where both the depth and the duration of the peak to trough movement are thus by definition underestimated). The data suggest that the stronger the trade collapse the longer the rebound: the difference in the extent of collapse is 1.5 percentage points. The difference between the duration of the trade collapse for those countries where the import volume is improving (4.6 quarters) and where the imports are still deteriorating (5.0 quarters) is small but statistically and economically meaningful.

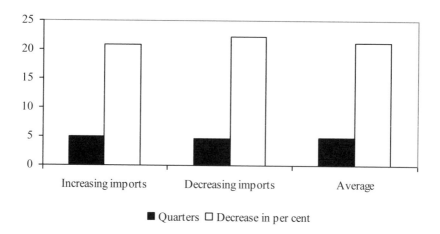

Note: For Australia, the Czech Republic, Denmark, Luxembourg, Mexico, New Zealand and
          Russia: 2009Q2

*Figure 2.2   Development of import volume 2007Q4–2009Q3 for two
             subgroups (35 countries, peak to trough, seasonally adjusted)*

Identification and Timing

The identification of the timing and extent of the trade collapse, moreover, is by no means easy and straightforward and would seem to depend to a large extent on the moment of observation. This is a relevant problem for this book which is written in the midst of the world trade collapse. Consider Figure 2.3, which shows the development of the import volumes of Ireland, Norway and the United Kingdom according to National Accounts data that were available at the end of 2009. Identifying the 'import business cycle' is relatively straightforward for the case of the United Kingdom: a clear and unambiguous peak (a local maximum) occurs in the fourth quarter of 2007 (although it should be noted that the difference with the adjacent quarters is less than half a per cent). Also the turning point in the import volume collapse can be identified without a lot of problems as the partial recovery unambiguously occurs in the second quarter of 2009.

The identification of the peak in the case of Norway, however, is not without difficulties. The fourth quarter of 2007 is the numerically correct moment, but eye-o-metrics suggests that the actual downturn starts in the third quarter of 2008 implying that the duration of the downturn may vary between five and three quarters. Likewise, while a trough (a local minimum) is observed in the first quarter of 2009, a downturn occurs again in the third quarter of 2009 (although the import volume does not decrease below the level of the first quarter of 2009 yet). If anything the data for Norway therefore illustrate the potentially problematic robustness of current assessments.

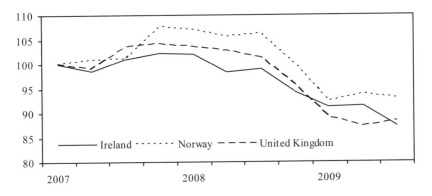

Source: OECD National Accounts

Figure 2.3   Import volume (index number 2007Q1=100) for Ireland,
Norway and the United Kingdom (2007Q1–2009Q3)

The fragility of analyses that use very recent data in the context of the world trade collapse is perhaps best illustrated by the case of the import volume of Ireland. We can date Ireland's peak import volume in the third quarter of 2007, but the difference with the first quarter of 2008 is only two percentage points, so measurement is again imprecise. The identification of the trough is even more problematic. In the third quarter of 2009 we would have measured a trough in the second quarter. In the second quarter of 2009 we would have measured the trough in the first quarter of 2009 (although the increase in the import volume was only three quarters of a percentage point), but at the start of 2010 the most recently available data showed that the trough may only have been reached in the third quarter of 2009, but this is by no means certain of course. The implication is that both the duration and the depth of the trade collapse may be underestimated by the currently available data. In the case of Ireland the duration varies between an optimistic two to three quarters and an estimate of an ongoing downturn of at least seven quarters. The concomitant decreases of the Irish import volume vary between 4 and 15 (or more) per cent.

2. WHY IMPORT RATHER THAN EXPORT IS KEY TO UNDERSTANDING THE TRADE COLLAPSE

It is important to point out that in contrast to most economists and policy makers this book will be concerned with the analysis of imports rather than exports.[2] There are essentially four reasons for my focus on imports.

Imports Versus Exports

First of all, the focus on exports as a driver of national welfare is misplaced. It is true that in the national accounts exports add to national income while imports are subtracted, but this is purely static bookkeeping that neglects the dynamic impact of imports and their importance for economic growth over the longer term. The focus on exports is a remainder of mercantilist thinking. In a nutshell mercantilism can be seen as a set of beliefs and policy prescriptions that maximize the surplus on the balance of trade in order to earn the means that are deemed necessary for warfare (Schumpeter 1954, pp. 364–7). A key element of this theory is the vision on trade as a zero sum game which implies that surpluses on one's trade balance are to the detriment of other countries and thus reduce their capacity to arm themselves and wage war and *vice versa*. Modern mercantilism is more sophisticated and less prone to wage wars, but the key idea that export is better than import can be recognized in many theories and policies. This is simply wrong: just as consumption is the ultimate goal of production, it is import that is the ultimate goal of export. Indeed, economic growth requires imports of capital goods, raw materials, intermediate goods and essential consumer goods.

Secondly, the development of a country's exports is largely determined by factors that at least in the short run are often exogenous to its firms and policy makers. Key drivers include import demand by trading partners (which amongst others depends on the state of their economy) or the imposition of tariffs and non-tariff barriers or other forms of protectionism by other countries. In contrast imports can be influenced by parameters that are in the national decision making domain. In addition to the key drivers mentioned, the allocation of credit and the use of domestic taxes and subsidies provide the means to influence the level of one's imports in the short run.

Thirdly, it is a waste of observations if one only studies the development of exports as is often done. Actually, we can learn a lot more from the development of imports during individual financial crises, essentially because the development of exports to a large extent is exogenous and – given the often mercantilist view of policy makers – may be sheltered from any negative consequences of the financial crisis. The impact of an individual financial crisis may thus be observed more accurately and directly when one studies the development of the volume of imports. This approach therefore provides a basis for comparison that can put the recent collective financial crisis into perspective.

This brings us to the final reason to study imports. During a global crisis all countries experience contractions of their effective demand and thus global import demand contracts as well. In this case the short side rule applies: the size of world markets during a global crisis is not determined by supply but by demand, that is: world trade is determined by the imports of all countries.

It is amongst others this perspective on the importance of imports – left out of many recent analyses and policy discussions – that I want to provide in this book. Recent studies provide ample evidence that justifies this approach as we will see in Section 3.

The Ambiguous Impact on Exports in Individual Financial Crises

The reason for the neglect of trade in most analyses of the aftermath of financial crises may very well be that the impact of a crisis on exports is ambiguous. The decline in domestic demand may induce firms to find new markets abroad and, if so, exports may *increase* during a financial crisis. Moreover, policy makers may respond with competitive devaluations of the currency so that one could also expect that exports will increase in the aftermath of a financial crisis (Fingerand and Schuknecht, 1999, p. 24). More importantly, individual country experiences during such episodes typically show that many policy makers opt for an export-led growth strategy to get out of the crisis situation. Resources are often re-allocated towards the export sector in order to ensure that hard currency can be earned, for example, in order to be able to meet international debt obligations. Also on this account exports may tend to grow during and after financial crises.

Given this theoretical ambiguity it is not surprising that the available empirical evidence regarding the impact of financial crises on export growth is mixed. The seminal study by Claessens et al. (2008) provides an empirical description for 21 OECD countries over the period 1960–2007. One finding is that the median export growth rate remains positive over the cycle for the majority of observations. Only in the lowest quartile do exports show a short dip of less than 5 per cent. Claessens et al. (2008, Tables 7, 8, 9 and 11, pp. 66–70) also provide detailed tabulations for different kinds of recessions (that is crises associated with a credit crunch, house price busts, equity price busts and oil price shocks, respectively) in order to investigate whether the observations for a specific kind of crisis differ from the average full sample pattern. They generally report insignificant coefficients so that we may conclude that the patterns reported are representative for the OECD experience.[3]

Table 2.2 Export volumes and banking crises in 36 emerging markets (1980–2005)

	Manufacturing exporters	Non-oil commodity exporters
Exports volume lagged[a]	0.85[***]	0.89[***]
Relative price	−0.17[***]	0.01
Lagged	0.10[*]	−0.01
Income	1.39[***]	1.51[***]
Lagged	−1.06[*]	−1.3[*]
Banking crisis dummy	−0.013[*]	−0.039[*]
Lagged	0.00	0.01
Private capital flows[b]	0.03	0.28
Lagged	1.48[***]	1.27[***]
Number of observations	523	279
Number of countries	22	12
R^2	0.98	0.97

Notes: [a] Variables are contemporaneous unless otherwise indicated

[b] Emerging market private capital flows in per cent of recipient's GDP

[*] Significant at 90 per cent confidence level

[**] Significant at 95 per cent confidence level

[***] Significant at 99 per cent confidence level

Source: Based on Thomas (2009), Table 2, p. 7

Thomas (2009, Tables 2, p. 7, and A2, p. 10) estimates traditional export equations for 34 emerging middle income economies in the years 1980–2005. To these equations – which relate the volume of exports to measures of relative prices and domestic and foreign income (that is real GDP) – Thomas adds a binary dummy variable which assumes the value 1 for years that a banking crisis occurs in the emerging market economy.[4] Splitting the sample between manufacturing exporters and non-oil commodity exporters, Thomas reports a negative contemporaneous banking crisis dummy (see Table 2.2). This dummy variable is significant for the exports of emerging markets that are hit by a financial crisis (but only at the 90 per cent confidence level and in some non-reported specifications the coefficient is even below this threshold). Depending on the specification his findings imply that export volumes fall by 1.3 to 3.9 per cent in countries that experience a domestic banking crisis.

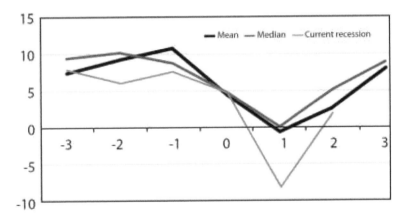

Source: Hong et al. (2009, Figure 3, p. 14)

Figure 2.4 Development of exports of 21 developing countries in Asia in per cent

Hong et al. (2009, Figure 3, p. 14) graphically report an average slowdown of export growth. Their findings that relate to 21 developing Asian economies and the years 1967–2007 are reproduced in Figure 2.4.[5] The figure plots the growth rate of exports for three years before and after a peak year (which is denoted by 0). Their forecast for the current recession (that is for the years 2009 and 2010; years 1 and 2 in Figure 2.4) is a real reduction of exports in 2009 which is different from the general average pattern. Note that Hong et al. base their 'current recession projection' on Economist Intelligence Unit (EIU) forecasts, which are available only for the limited sample of Hong

Kong, Korea, Malaysia, Papua New Guinea, Philippines, Singapore and Thailand. More important is that both the mean and median response in their full sample never become significantly negative, implying that the overall pattern is that exports during recessions in Asia do not tend to decrease on average. Freund (2009b) analyses trade data for four global downturns (defined as sharp drops of annual world real production growth below 2 per cent) in 1975, 1982, 1991 and 2001. In addition she investigates three major cases of banking crises (Finland, Japan and Sweden in the 1990s). For these cases Freund (2009b, p. 9) finds a much stronger fall of the level of imports and also that 'Exports fell by just the same amount as world trade, suggesting that the aggregate exports of the crisis countries were no more affected by global downturn than exports in the rest of the world.' Iacovone and Zavacka (2009a and 2009b) have analysed the issue at a disaggregated level of 81 sectors (the 4 digit ISTC level) finding a significant decrease in the rate of export growth of about 4 per cent in sectors that depend highly on bank finance. Importantly, however, they study only banking crises that do not include a collapse of the currency and their results at the level of individual sectors cannot be translated into a number for the decrease of the growth rate of total exports (which in all likelihood is smaller than the quoted four per cent figure).

The evidence regarding the development of exports during a recession is all in all inconclusive, which seems to imply that export is not strongly impacted during a financial crisis. Indeed, the IMF (2009a, p. 112) notes that

> one key factor that helped economies recover from a recession associated with a financial crisis was the fact that they were able to benefit from strong external demand. This suggests that disruptions to the supply of credit may not matter much for firms that are highly dependent on outside funding if they produce goods that are highly tradable.

This stylized fact, however, should not lead to the erroneous conclusion that finance is not important for international trade. On the contrary, the disruption of credit *a priori* would seem to be very relevant for international trade, be it for import flows or for export flows, as we will see in Chapter 3 (and it is important to add that payment risk may be especially relevant for the importer who will experience a rise in transaction costs, for example, because letters of credit or even full payment in advance is required).

From a political economy perspective, moreover, the perception may be relevant that imports entail an outflow of hard currency. Thus policy makers might not be inclined to come to the aid of importing firms (unless the imports are crucial for the exporting industry). The reduction in effective demand that is a consequence of a financial crisis directly translates into a reduced import volume. Finally, in a scenario that involves a depreciation of the currency the price of imports will rise and thus exert a negative influence on the volume of imports. All in all the impact of a financial crisis should be expected to be most visible and unambiguous in the development of the volume of imports and this is the issue of the next section.

3. A SHORT HISTORY OF FINANCIAL CRISES AND IMPORT CRUNCHES (1980–2006)

Figure 2.5 summarizes the depth (percentage decrease) and duration (quarters) of the reduction of imports. These variables are measured from peak (that is the turning point where the rate of growth of imports becomes negative) to trough (that is the end of the contraction of the import volume where the rate of growth becomes positive again). Figure 2.5 deals with the aftermath of 18 important financial crises that were identified in Fingerand and Schuknecht (1999) and Reinhart and Rogoff (2009). These crises occurred after 1980 and before 2007, the year that the credit crisis set in.

My sample of 18 crises is more balanced than other studies in the sense that this group of countries covers most continents and includes countries with rather different levels of development. The sample is biased because relative small financial crises are not included and because a lack of reliable data prohibited the inclusion of all crises studied in Fingerand and Schuknecht (1999) and Reinhart and Rogoff (2009). Moreover, the comparability of the data is imperfect since different sources had to be consulted so that the real reductions in the volume of imports are based on different methodologies. Only in a limited number of cases were the preferred data (import volumes deflated by relevant price indices) available from the IMF. So other methods had to be used as well, for example, National Accounts data which are available from the OECD or the IMF and which are deflated by import price indices (that are established on a national basis) or by the GDP deflator. The imperfectness of the data is a practical problem that, unfortunately, cannot be solved if one wants to broaden the perspective and thus has to study a group of heterogeneous countries as in this book. Clearly thus the results need to be interpreted with caution. (The appendix to this chapter provides details on the sources and methods that have been used for individual countries.)

Findings and Relevancy

With this caveat in mind it is noteworthy that the volume of imports on average decreased by 25.4 per cent (with a standard deviation of 13.4) during 4.8 quarters (with a standard deviation of 2.6).

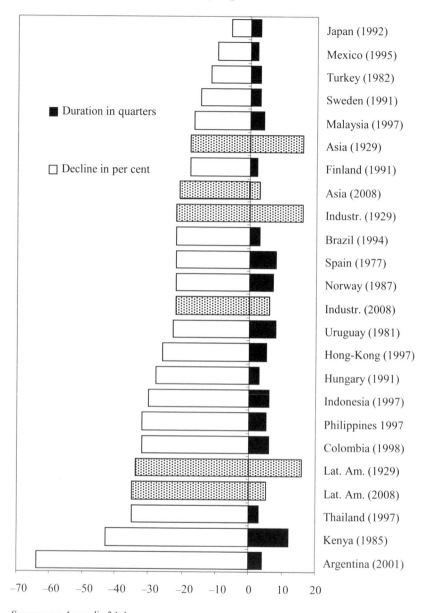

Sources: see Appendix 2A.1

Figure 2.5   *Development of import volumes during 18 post-1980 financial crises, (grey bars relate to during the 1930s and since 2007) (peak-to-trough decrease in per cent and duration in quarters)*

This is much in line with the findings for the world trade recessions analysed by Faber and Van Marrewijk (2009), who find an average duration of 14 months in their analysis of world trade for the period 1991–2007. Araújo and Oliveira Martins (2009) report an average duration of 13 months in OECD trade for the years 1965–2009. Typically this would seem to imply that a normal trade cycle would turn upward again at the end of 2009 or the beginning of 2010. One remaining issue that can only be solved by the passage of time is of course whether the 2008–2009 trade collapse was normal in this sense or whether the '2008–201?' trade collapse is a special class also regarding its duration.

Anyhow, the empirical evidence summarized in Figure 2.5 can also be compared to the findings in the studies of Claessens et al. (2008), Thomas (2009) and Hong et al. (2009), which were introduced and discussed in Section 2 of the present chapter.

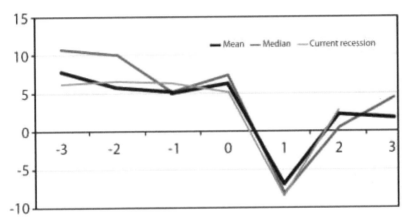

Source: Hong et al. (2009, Figure 3, p. 14)

Figure 2.6 Development of imports of 21 developing countries in Asia in per cent

Claessens et al. (2008, pp. 46 and 66–70), depending on the type of the crisis that is being studied, report for their sample of 122 recessions in 21 OECD countries in the years 1960–2007 that median and mean decreases in import volumes occur in the range of –5 to –8 per cent. The median import growth becomes negative during three quarters (in the lowest quartile the duration of the import reduction is seven quarters). Only in the upper quartile does the import growth rate remain positive although it also shows a strong dip. The smaller amplitude for OECD countries is in line with the fact that generally speaking the largest impacts according to Figure 2.5 are found in

non-OECD countries. Thomas (2009, Tables 1, p. 4 and A1, p. 9) finds a
contraction of about 2 per cent at a 90 per cent confidence level in import
demand equations estimated for 38 emerging middle income economies in the
years 1980–2005. Figure 2.6 reports the findings by Hong et al. (2009)
regarding the average impact of a financial crisis in 21 Asian developing
countries in the years 1967–2007 and consistently shows a negative growth
rate in the order of magnitude of 5–10 per cent.

*Table 2.3 Duration of the import crunch and its recovery (18 major post-
            1980 financial crises)*

	Year	Period (Quarters)	
		Peak to trough	Recovery to pre-crisis level
Uruguay	1981	8	32
Kenya	1985	12	28
Colombia	1998	6	20
Norway	1987	7	16
Finland	1991	2	15
Argentine	2001	4	13
Hongkong	1997	5	13
Philippines	1997	5	13
Spain	1977	8	13
Thailand	1997	3	13
Indonesie	1997	6	12
Sweden	1991	3	12
Brazil	1994	3	8
Malaysia	1997	4	8
Japan	1992	3	7
Hungary	1991	3	6
Mexico	1995	2	3
Turkey	1982	3	3

Sources: see Appendix 2A.1

Again the conclusion of this overview is that the studies agree that a normal
trade recession lasts about five quarters. It is important to note that this peak-
to-trough development may provide a distorted and a too optimistic picture of
the actual duration of the problems. At the trough the rate of import growth
turns positive and this indicates of course that trade is no longer collapsing.
By itself this is good news, but that does not mean that the *status quo ante* has
been restored. An economic variable may need many years of positive growth

rates before a collapse is completely overcome. Consider, for example, Table 2.3 which for the same sample of 18 financial crises analysed in Figure 2.5 provides further information on the length of the recovery, that is the time that elapses until the import volume has completely returned to its pre-crisis level. Recovery to pre-crisis levels on average takes 13.1 quarters (with a standard deviation of 7.6). Often the cases appear to be of a long and protracted nature. Moreover, it is not obvious that one can rely upon a generalization of these individual cases.

Duration is an Important Remaining Issue

What does this all imply for the recent world trade collapse? As you will have noted Figure 2.5 also contains three regional averages (Asia, Industrialized Countries and Latin America) for the 1930s and the post 2007 period. The figure makes a few points. Firstly, the decrease in per cent during the first year of the 2008–2009 trade collapse is already comparable with the experience in the 1930s. Secondly, the key difference between the individual financial crises and the collective crisis of the interbellum appears to occur in the duration of the import crunch as the regional import volumes in the 1930s decreased over a period of four years (so 16 quarters; the available data are annual data). Thirdly, actual recovery to pre-crisis regional trade levels took some eight years. For most countries trade volumes did not even fully recover before the Second World War. So by the end of December 2009 on the basis of the available data one could conclude that the depth of the import crunch was in line with both the 1930s and the individual crises in the 1980s and 1990s. The key difference with the earlier phenomena was the duration of the peak to trough movement. With the duration of the import collapse at the average of the 18 post-1980/pre-2007 financial crises the world economy appeared to be at a watershed early 2010. World trade could rebound, but also move into uncharted territory where the only point of reference would be the 1930s. It is time to take a closer look at these periods.

4. INDIVIDUAL COUNTRY EXPERIENCES IN THE 1930s AND IN 2007–2009

As already observed in Chapter 1 a high level of aggregation may obscure the extent to which one can identify the occurrence and depth of trade collapses. At the individual level much more details are available than for the highly aggregated world trade level. This is why this section studies the first and second trade collapse at the level of individual countries.

Table 2.4 Countries that recovered from the import crunch, 1921–1938

Country	Peak	Recovery	Recovery period (years)
Australia	1927	1938	11
Finland	1928	1935	7
Japan	1929	1933	4
New Zealand	1929	1936	7
Norway	1930	1936	6
South Africa	1929	1939	5
Sweden	1931	1935	4
Taiwan	1932	1935	3
USA	1929	1937	8

Sources: Maddison (1985), Tables A-6, p. 87 and A-12, p. 90 and United Nations Statistical
Office (1962), Tables II –XXIII

The 1930s

Table 2.4 is based on a group of 27 countries for which real import volume
data are available for the interbellum. Only nine countries (that is one third)
were able to recover their import level before the Second World War.[6]

Unfortunately my data sources do not cover 1939 probably because of the
usual secrecy that surrounds the advent of war, but it is reasonable to assume
that if the trade flows had occurred to previous peak levels in 1939 that this
would have been due to the war efforts and not to business cycle processes.
Therefore the exclusion of 1939 from the data does not seriously distort the
analysis of real import development of individual countries during the
interbellum.

Figure 2.7 in addition, provides a detailed individual account of depth and
duration for the full sample of 27 countries. The depth of the import reduction
ranges from −4 per cent for Japan to an astonishing −82 per cent in the case
of Chile. The duration of the peak to trough movement varies between one
year for the United Kingdom and nine years for Germany. Average depth in
this sample for 27 countries in the 1930s is −43 per cent (with a standard
deviation of 17). This is a 15 percentage points larger decrease in the volume
of trade than observed in the previous section for the 18 recent individual
financial crises of the pre-2007 period. In the interbellum we observe an
average duration of 4.3 year (17 quarters or 52 months) with a standard
deviation of 1.9. Indeed, this is well in excess of any trade recession observed
in the post-Second World War era.

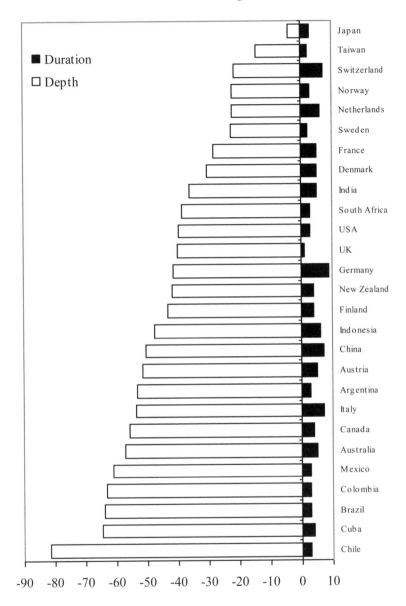

Sources: Maddison (1985) Tables A-6, p. 87 and A-12, p. 90 and United Nations Statistical
Office (1962), Tables II –XXIII (see also the data appendix)

*Figure 2.7 Development of import volumes during the 1930s (measured
peak to trough, depth per cent and duration in years)*

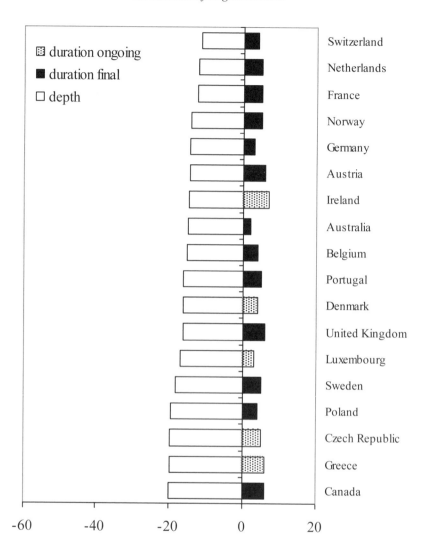

Note: For Australia, the Czech Republic, Denmark, Luxembourg, Mexico, New Zealand and
           Russia: 2009Q2

*Figure 2.8   Depth in per cent and duration in quarters of the import crunch
              for 35 individual countries (2007–2009Q3) distinguished by
              countries for which the crunch was ongoing and countries for
              which a turning point appears to have been reached*

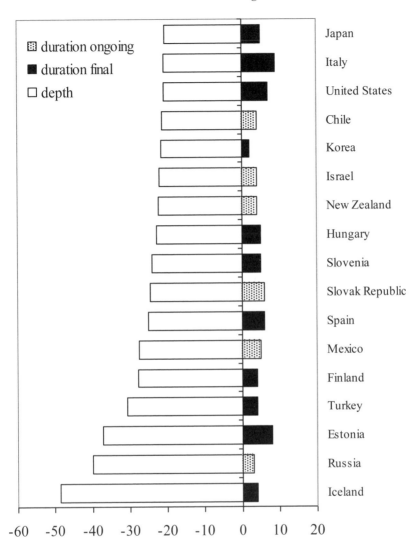

Figure 2.8 (continued)

Developments Since 2007

The 2008–2009 world trade collapse appears to have occurred (at least initially) at much larger speed than happened in the 1930s. In less than half a year a reduction in the volume of world trade by some 20 per cent could be observed, whereas the collapse took some four years during the Great

Depression. The question of the duration of the recent world trade collapse is still open but we can already glean the trade destruction that took place in the three years before 2010.

Figure 2.8 describes the data available at the start of 2010 for a group of 35 countries that are available from the OECD National Account Statistics. My choice to use this data source is pragmatic: the delay in the publication is short, the data are relatively good in the sense that they are produced by reliable statistical agencies using well-established methods. The data are seasonally adjusted and constructed for national accounting purposes.

The figure distinguishes between countries (black bars) where the import volume was increasing again before or by the end of the third quarter of 2009 and countries (grey bars) where it was still decreasing (and where both the depth and the duration of the peak to trough movement are thus by definition underestimated). The depth of the import trough ranges from −11 per cent for Switzerland to −49 per cent for Iceland. The average depth for the 35 countries is −21 per cent (with a standard deviation of 8) and the average duration is five quarters (with a standard deviation of 1.5).

The average percentage decrease in the import volume exceeds the findings in section 3 but remains well below the average impact reported in Figure 2.7. All in all the reported depth exceeds the official projections for 2009 and 2010 (Table 2.1) but the duration is actually still more or less in line with the expectations of the international organizations that trade will show positive growth in 2010.

5. CONCLUSIONS

It is useful to summarize the different findings for the three periods that we have considered: the 1930s, the quarter of a century preceding the financial crisis that started in 2007 and the recent period of trade collapse.

It is important to note that a synthesis over a period of some 80 years is difficult because national borders have been redrawn: some countries disappeared, others emerged and again others do not cover the same geographic area anymore. It is also important that the data sources differ and that measurement methods and data collection processes must have changed over this long period. Clearly the table needs to be interpreted with caution, but with that caveat in mind Table 2.5 may still provide some interesting observations.

Firstly, it is noteworthy that five countries have been included in the data sets that have been analysed in this chapter: Finland, Japan, Mexico, Norway and Sweden. These countries were important trading countries in the 1930s. They were OECD member countries during the recent world trade collapse.

Finally all five experienced a severe financial crisis in the period 1980−2006. Figures 2.9 and 2.10 show for the three periods concerned the depth and duration, respectively. (Note that the five countries appeared to have reached the turning point in the import cycle by the third quarter of 2009.)

Table 2.5 Summary table for depth in per cent and duration in quarters for countries that appear at least twice in the analysis

	1930s		1980–2006		2007–2009	
	Depth	Duration	Depth	Duration	Depth	Duration
Argentina	−53	12	−64	4		
Australia	−57	20			−15	2
Austria	−51	20			−15	6
Brazil	−64	12	−22	3		
Canada	−56	16			−20	6
Chile	−81	12			−21	4*
Colombia	−63	12	−32	6		
Denmark	−30	20			−16	4*
Finland	−43	16	−18	2	−28	4
France	−28	20			−12	5
Germany	−41	36			−14	3
Hungary			−28	3	−23	5
Indonesia	−48	24	−30	6		
Italy	−53	28			−21	9
Japan	−4	12	−6	3	−20	5
Mexico	−61	12	−10	2	−28	5*
Netherlands	−22	24			−12	5
New Zealand	−42	16			−22	4*
Norway	−22	12	−22	7	−14	5
Spain			−22	8	−25	6
Sweden	−23	8	−15	3	−18	5
Switzerland	−22	28			−11	4
Taiwan	−14	8	−35	3		
Turkey			−12	3	−31	4
UK	−40	4			−16	6
USA	−40	12			−21	7
Lowest	−81	4	−64	2	−31	2
Highest	−4	36	−6	8	−11	9

Note: * Duration not definitely established on the basis of 2009Q3 data

Figures 2.9 and 2.10 show that the current crisis in terms of both depth and duration has had a stronger impact thant the individual financial crises of the 1980s and 1990s – Norway is the exception in this regard – but also that the 1930s with no exception were characterized by substantially larger movements from peak to trough over much longer periods. In this sense the trade collapses in the twentieth and twenty-first centuries appear to be of quite different magnitudes. It will be interesting to investigate why the two trade collapses differ. This may be due to structural differences (for example the composition of trade) and/or to policy difference. Both factors will be investigated further in the next chapters.

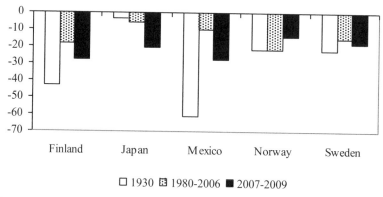

Figure 2.9   *The real percentage decrease of the import volume for Finland, Japan, Mexico, Norway and Sweden in the 1930s, 1980–2006 and 2007–2009*

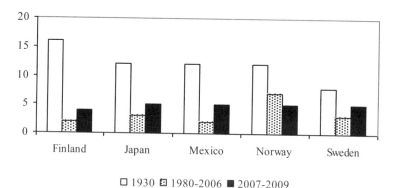

Figure 2.10   *The duration of the real import decrease in quarters for Finland, Japan, Mexico, Norway and Sweden in the 1930s, 1980–2006 and 2007–2009*

Secondly, Table 2.5 shows the large and historically diverging variations that exist for the depth of the crises. In the 1930s the largest decrease is twenty times larger than the smallest observation. In the individual crises since 1980 this amounts to a factor of ten and during the recent crisis the factor is three. The variation in duration is a bit smaller with the 1930s again witnessing the largest spread (a factor of nine) and the other periods having the same manner of variation (the factor is four). The differences in the extent of variation observed in the three periods, however, should not obscure the key common stylized fact, that is that individual country experiences differ a lot even for the relatively homogeneous set of OECD countries in the years following 2007. Tanaka (2009) has also pointed out the fact that the trade contraction has differed markedly across industrial countries and that 'this asymmetric fall in trade is not correlated with exposure to the crisis in any simple and straightforward way'. Levchenko et al. (2009, p. 12) argue that

> In both developed countries and emerging markets, there appears to be a great deal of heterogeneity (...). This is in spite of the fact that international trade itself collapsed in all (...) countries. This suggests that behind the superficial similarity in country experience, there is important heterogeneity in the underlying shocks and transmission mechanisms. Sorting out this variation remains a fruitful direction for future research.

The key conclusion of this chapter is therefore that it is very important to understand why these country experiences diverge, and this is the task set for the next chapters.

NOTES

[1] Compare Figure 1.6. The full recovery of the 1930s in this sense takes until the mid-1970s.

[2] See, however, Iacovone and Zavacka (2009a and b) for a comparable analysis of the development of exports during a set of banking crises in a comparable period that is being studied in this chapter

[3] Only in recessions that include house price bursts is the impact on the volume of exports significantly different at the 90 per cent confidence level; the coefficient is positive.

[4] For manufacturing exporters the relative price is the export deflator divided by the unit labour costs of trading partners and for non-oil commodity exporters it is the world non-oil commodity price index divided by the exporter's Consumer Price Index.

[5] Their sample covers the ASEAN countries (Brunei, Burma, Cambodia, Indonesia, Laos, Malaysia, Philippines, Singapore, Thailand and Vietnam), Bangladesh, the People's Republic of China, Hong Kong, China, India, Kazakhstan, the Republic

of Korea, the Kyrgyz Republic, Pakistan, Papua New Guinea, Sri Lanka and Uzbekistan

6　Korea had a small setback in its import trade volume in 1931 but stayed well ahead of levels in previous years. Moreover, the country was on a healthy growth trajectory over the whole interbellum and is for that reason not included in the analysis.

Appendix 2A1: Data Sources

This appendix provides two detailed lists of data sources by country for those parts of the analysis in Chapter 2 where the data set had to be created using different sources and often different definitions of variables (including the use of different price deflators). Typically these parts of the analysis aim at analysing as large a group of individual countries as possible and for that reason the use of different sources was unavoidable.

Data Sources for Figure 2.5 and Table 2.3

Argentina (2001): IMF, *International Financial Statistics (IFS)*, index number import volume.

Asia (1929): Regional average in Maddison (1985), Table 2, p. 14.

Brazil (1994): IMF, *IFS*, imports in constant prices.

Colombia (1998), IMF, *IFS*, imports in current prices deflated by GDP deflator.

Finland (1991) *OECD Quarterly National Accounts*, seasonally adjusted index number volume imports.

Hongkong (1997): IMF, *IFS*, index number import volume.

Hungary (1991): IMF, *IFS*, imports in constant prices.

Indonesia (1997): IMF, *IFS*, imports in current prices deflated by GDP deflator.

Industrialized countries (1929): Regional average in Maddison (1985), Table 1, p. 13.

Japan (1992): IMF, *IFS*, index number import volume.

Kenya (1985): Fingerand and Schuknecht (1999), p. 42.

Latin America (1929): Regional average in Maddison (1985), Table 2, p. 14.

Malaysia (1997): IMF, *IFS*, imports in current prices deflated by GDP deflator.

Mexico (1995): IMF, *IFS*, imports in current prices deflated by GDP deflator.

Norway (1987): IMF, *IFS*, index number import volume.

Philippines (1997): IMF, *IFS*, index number import volume.

Spain (1977): IMF, *IFS*, imports in current prices deflated by GDP deflator.

Sweden (1991): IMF, *IFS*, index number import volume.

Thailand (1997): IMF, *IFS*, index number import volume.

Turkey (1982): IMF, *IFS*, index number import volume.

Uruguay (1981): IMF, *IFS*, imports in current prices deflated by GDP deflator.

Data Sources for Figure 2.7 and Table 2.4

Argentina: Maddison (1985), Table A6, p. 87.
Australia: United Nations Statistical Office (1962), Table III.
Austria: United Nations Statistical Office (1962), Table IV.
Brazil: Maddison (1985), Table A6, p. 87.
Canada: United Nations Statistical Office (1962), Table VII.
Chile: United Nations Statistical Office (1962), Table VIII.
China: Maddison (1985), Table A12, p. 90.
Colombia: Maddison (1985), Table A6, p. 87.
Cuba: Maddison (1985), Table A6, p. 87.
Denmark: United Nations Statistical Office (1962), Table IX.
Finland: United Nations Statistical Office (1962), Table X.
France: United Nations Statistical Office (1962), Table XI.
Germany: United Nations Statistical Office (1962), Table XII.
India: United Nations Statistical Office (1962), Table XIII.
Indonesia: Maddison (1985), Table A12, p. 90.
Italy: United Nations Statistical Office (1962), Table XIV.
Japan: United Nations Statistical Office (1962), Table XV.
Mexico: Maddison (1985), Table A6, p. 87.
Netherlands: United Nations Statistical Office (1962), Table XVI.
New Zealand: United Nations Statistical Office (1962), Table XVII.
Norway: United Nations Statistical Office (1962), Table XVII.
South Africa: United Nations Statistical Office (1962), Table XIX.
Sweden: United Nations Statistical Office (1962), Table XX.
Switzerland: United Nations Statistical Office (1962), Table XXI.
United Kingdom: United Nations Statistical Office (1962), Table XXII.
United States: United Nations Statistical Office (1962), Table XXIII.

3. The Trade Finance Confusion: Tales of Capital, Finance, Credit and Trade

In the very early phase of the trade collapse observers already pointed to trade finance as one of the culprits for the significant reductions in import and export volumes. That reaction should not have come as a surprise. With credit in short supply and banks in serious trouble, trade finance could have been expected to decline sharply as had happened in other financial crises. One of the positive consequences of the Asia crisis that occurred in the second half of the 1990s had been the greater awareness of policy makers with respect to the vulnerability of trade finance in times of crisis and, consequently, of imports and exports that to a large extent depend on trade finance.[1] Auboin (2009b) provides a relevant and interesting historical account of the international co-operation in the context of G20 and WTO policy preparation of working groups of international experts on this topic that emerged in the slipstream of the Asia and Dotcom crises. The networks of policy makers and procedures for international co-operation and assessment by experts have their roots in the collapse of trade credit during these periods.[2] The world trade collapse revitalized the co-operation and this formed an important basis for policy initiatives by the G20 and the international institutions to support trade finance.

In a sense policy makers were very well prepared to focus on collapsing trade financing as a cause of de-globalization when actual trade flows showed an unprecedented breakdown (both in terms of percentage decreases and the speed at which these occurred). But were the trade analysts in the international organizations right? Or was this merely a case of policy analysts that were trying to absolve a pre-cooked policy recipe? Was trade finance an issue that politicians could be interested in because trade finance is a way to help national exporting firms? Was this perhaps a topic where visible gestures were possible at small costs?

These are nagging questions, indeed. It is important to note that there were actually no data to check whether this idea made any sense at all. In 2004 the Bank of International Settlement (BIS) had discontinued its trade finance series. Those statistical series had been co-produced by BIS, IMF, OECD and World Bank and according to Auboin (2009b, p.11) 'the cost-to-quality ratio of these statistics led the agencies to discontinue this effort'. This was very unfortunate since the only remaining source for time series thus was the Berne Union data base which only covered a specific part of the industry, namely trade credit insurance. Given that no real time data were available in early 2009, one is led to the conclusion that senior policy makers and senior analysts basically appear to have sincerely *believed* that a trade finance squeeze was taking place but the evidence on which their convictions were based can only have been anecdotal at best. Later on a number of surveys were organized, but this could not provide the full picture as we will discuss in Section 4 below.

This chapter will take a critical look at the two essential questions: Why does financial turbulence matter for trade? and, Did the development of trade finance really matter for the trade collapse that started at the end of 2008? If we want to answer these questions we need to discuss some theories and then also involve empirical matters. It is, moreover, important to make distinctions between different kinds of financial flows. In Section 2 we will be dealing with foreign direct investment (FDI). Section 3 focuses on theories related to trade finance (that is financial relations between banks and firms) and to trade credit (that is intra-firm financial relations), respectively. Section 4 provides a detailed discussion of empirical findings that appear to have shaped the policy debate. Section 5 draws some conclusions and provides an overview of policy initiatives and attempts to assess their appropriateness as a response to the trade collapse.

1. THE TRADE–FINANCE NEXUS

Before we start a discussion on different types of capital and credit, however, it should be noted that the idea that finance and the trade collapse are interlinked *a priori* would seem to make a lot of sense. Typically, during a financial crisis a concomitant credit crunch occurs that hits all sectors of an economy. The financial instability will have a relative strong impact on the more risky sectors because the risk appetite of banks, other financial intermediaries and capital providers decreases sharply during (and often also in the years following) a financial crisis. This reduction in the availability of credit for firms and consumers is one of the driving forces behind the contraction of economic activity.

International activities are ceteris paribus more risky than local activities which can be observed more readily and do not involve a number of risks that are relevant for international transactions such as the risks that a country will no longer honour its payment obligations, repudiate its debt, nationalize foreign assets and/or devalue the currency. Typically, international bank lending to private firms and governments as well as cross-border portfolio and direct investment decrease during financial crises and the financial crisis that started in 2007 is no exception to this empirical regularity. Moreover, like in the 1930s tight credit conditions spread to developing countries, and this was even true for types of credit and institutions (such as micro finance; see Box 3.1) that many observers had assumed to be much less vulnerable to contagion by the problems of the industrialized countries.[3]

Box 3.1 The unexpected contagion of micro credits

Moro Visconto (2009) argues – in line with Yunus' well known claim that 'micro finance still worked' (dated October 2, 2008) – in mid 2009 that micro finance is sound. Basically he uses *a priori* arguments, namely that micro finance institutions were only involved in real transactions (so there was no detachment between the real and the financial valuation of transactions, had no toxic assets, and were less vulnerable for the usual influence of the business cycle on repayment behaviour because the activities mainly related to personal services and small businesses in the informal sector while funding was largely socially motivated. Based on a questionnaire for 84 micro finance institutions, however, Huisman and Lensink (2009) report deteriorating repayment behaviour and higher cost of capital for about three quarters of the reviewed institutions.

Other unexpected victims of the financial crisis appear to have been the flow of remittances of immigrant workers to their home country and official development aid flows (World Bank 2009c; UNCTAD 2009e and OECD 2010). During the early 2000s remittances had been assumed to be much less unstable and actually independent of business cycle developments and had shown very substantial increases, but the financial crisis and the expected negative impact on immigrants, their wages and employment changed the appreciation for this manner of capital flow. Regarding development aid, it appeared to be very unfortunate that commitments, targets and/or norms had been formulated in the past as a percentage of the donor's national income. The recession in many donor countries thus led to a substantial deficit of aid flows with respect to earlier commitments if not real reductions of the volume of ODA.[4] In this spectre of decreasing international capital flows, two flows stand out as especially relevant because of their potentially strong impact on trade: FDI and trade credit (note that reductions of these respective capital flows may influence trade in opposite directions). FDI showed a much stronger contraction than trade finance and trade credit and this is interesting for two reasons. Firstly, it offers an empirical benchmark for the fall in trade finance and secondly, as FDI also reflects international interaction of firms it may offer a different and additional perspective on the process of deglobalization since 2008.

2. FOREIGN DIRECT INVESTMENT

The world FDI collapse was even more pronounced than the world trade collapse. UNCTAD's (2009b) *World Investment Prospects Survey* reported that 57 per cent of the multinationals expected a decrease in foreign direct investment and about half of them expected that this decrease would exceed the level of 30 per cent. The changed perspective on investment plans soon showed up in the international statistics.

The level of FDI fluctuated heavily on a quarter-to-quarter basis, but in addition FDI growth *vis-à-vis* the corresponding period in the previous year since the second quarter of 2008 consistently was in negative territory for the group of G20 countries (Figure 3.1). Negative growth rates were in the order of magnitude of −30 to −60 per cent.[5]

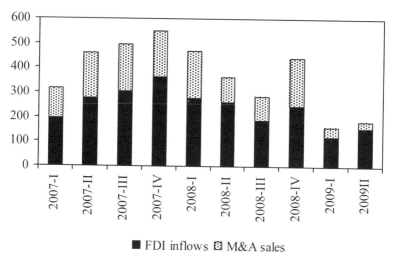

■ FDI inflows ▣ M&A sales

Note: Quarterly data are not available for Saudi Arabia
Source: Based on UNCTAD (2009d), Figure 2, p. 2

Figure 3.1 FDI inflows and cross-border mergers and acquisitions (billions of US dollars, G20-countries)

Not surprisingly, cross-border mergers and acquisitions (M&A) were fluctuating even more than foreign direct investment (the latter is defined in

international statistics as an investment that is made to acquire a lasting
interest in an enterprise operating in an economy other than that of the
investor, the investor's purpose being to have an effective voice in the
management of the enterprise – so one expects a more stable flow than for
mergers and acquisitions which are often driven by short-term rather than
strategic considerations). With regard to M&A, negative growth rates were
measured in the order of magnitude of −70 to −80 per cent in the first two
quarters of 2009. The total inflow of FDI and M&A may have bottomed out
early 2009, but UNCTAD (2009d, p. 2) pointed out two factors that
cautioned against optimism, namely the fact that 'the absolute level of FDI
flows was considerably larger than in the same period of 2008' and that

> the pick-up seemed to be mostly attributable to intra-company flows and
> reinvested earnings while equity flows remained unchanged and at a low level.
> This is a relevant finding, because equity flows are the FDI component that is most
> directly related to [a multinational's] longer-term investment strategy. So this
> finding would seem to suggest that multinational companies remained quite
> cautious during 2009 about their international expansion.

Accordingly UNCTAD did not expect a quick rebound. Figure 3.2 puts
these developments in a medium-term perspective. The FDI collapse exceeds
the decline during the Asia crisis, but note also the bottom of the investment
cycle still exceeds the levels that were observed in downturns during earlier
swings in FDI.

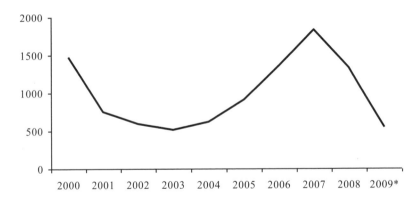

Note: * 2009 is the annualized number over the first half year available from UNCTAD (2009d)
Source: Based on UNCTAD (2009c), Figure 1.3, p. 5 and UNCTAD (2009d)

Figure 3.2   Global FDI inflows 2000–2009 (billions of US dollars)*

It is also important to note that a reduction in planned foreign direct investment may actually have offered some support to the volume of trade. Often FDI substitutes for exports, for example, when substantial trade barriers exist or when market access is hindered in other ways.[6] Setting up a production facility abroad may thus substitute for trade and possibly this process also works in the other direction. If so, the foreign direct investment squeeze may have reduced the decline of world trade.[7]

3. TRADE FINANCE AND TRADE CREDIT

It is useful to make a distinction between on the one hand, trade finance that relates to the involvement of banks and other financial institutions and on the other hand, trade credit where producers themselves provide credit to customers, either to other firms that use their products as intermediate inputs or to final consumers.

Table 3.1 The various risks of international exchange

Economic and commercial risks	Exchange rate risk	Transportation risk	Political risk
Importer unwilling or unable to pay	Variability (floating exchange rate regime)	Damage of goods	Foreign policy: war, embargoes and boycotts, restrictions for non-economic reasons (e.g. health policy)
Importer does not accept merchandise Exporter does not deliver on time or in other specification	De- or revaluation (fixed exchange rate)	Loss of goods	Domestic policy: revolt, civil war, consumer boycotts. Economic policy: currency inconvertibility, restrictions on transfers

International trade is a complex and risky activity with risks that are not relevant for domestic trade (such as exchange rate risk) or are *ceteris paribus* much larger (such as the transportation risks). Table 3.1 provides an overview. Domestic trade only has to deal with economic and commercial risks and the transportation risk (and of course one should read 'buyer' for 'importer' and seller for 'exporter'). Private insurance is available for many of these risks, but not for the political risks listed in the penultimate column of Table 3.1. Insurance against these country risks requires the involvement of the public sector (for example by means of government guarantees) and many countries have export credit agencies that provide public sector insurance against this manner of risk. Banks of course provide a lot of services that often include insurance of many risks as well as valuable information about local conditions and counter parties in foreign markets. Such banking services are vital for exporters and importers, but these activities will not be the topic of the discussions in this chapter as changes in these particular services would a priori seem to be less relevant as a driver for the collapse of trade. Instead we will focus on international finance by banks (in particular documentary credit and other forms of their pre- and post shipping financing activities). Trade finance should be distinguished from trade credit (such as bills of exchange, promissory notes, supplier credit and buyer credit) which is generally supplied by one of the trading partners without much involvement of the banking sector. Unfortunately this distinction is not always made in the literature, most likely because comprehensive and comparable data are not available for trade finance.[8] Many empirical researchers have thus tended to focus on trade credit (for which reliable time series are available for some countries, in particular the US) or have constructed macroeconomic measures of financial tightness that are assumed to represent the conditions on the market for trade finance.

The distinction between trade finance and trade credit is particularly relevant in situations that are characterized by shocks to the financial markets and financial sectors. During a financial crisis banks will reduce all lending activity, but firms may choose to step in themselves – even though they may also be credit constrained – in order to help their suppliers and customers. This substitution between the banking channel and the customer–supplier channel is not motivated by charity but by well understood self interest and efficiency considerations, as we will see. The point to remember, however, is that the substitution process may very well explain why it is difficult to detect an unambiguous relationship between trade on the one hand and finance and credit on the other hand.

Trade Credit

An interesting question is of course why non-financial firms would want to get involved in the process of supplying credits when specialized financial institutions such as banks and other financial intermediaries are available. Choi and Kim (2003) provide a useful review of theoretical considerations and explanations that may be relevant during a phase of trade collapse.[9]

Long-run supplier–customer relationships may provide a means to solve information problems because trading partners learn a lot about each other's business and also about their capacity to pay (or the capacity to service the debt that is inherent to any form of credit relationship). Suppliers may also be at an advantage *vis-à-vis* banks if payments are delayed because they can seize the goods (provided that the goods are in a country that recognizes the supplier's property rights, of course) and sell these goods to other clients in their customer base (for the supplier this is business as usual and banks may lack the specialized knowledge that is necessary to find potentially interested buyers). Trade credit suppliers may thus face lower transaction costs than banks. In addition to better knowledge and lower costs, firms often have an incentive to provide some form of credit to their customers as this instrument can be used to strengthen their competitive position and be used to offer a non-observable reduction in their price.

Trade Finance

Trade finance is often called the lifeblood of international trade because some 80–90 per cent of trade transactions require some form of guarantee, credit or insurance (Auboin 2009a). In comparison to other forms of international credit and investment, trade finance is, however, a low risk activity. Firstly, it is a short-term and essentially self-liquidating activity: the credit agreement is limited in time (it ends when the goods have been delivered and paid) and often also short-term in nature (up to half a year). Secondly, it is often a routine activity with many repeated transactions between exporters and importers which thus trust and know each other and their business conditions. Thirdly, the goods that are insured provide the actual collateral for the credit and although it is not always easy to seize collateral in different jurisdictions, mechanisms have been designed to ensure that goods are only transferred to the buyer if he or she is able to provide proof of payment. Banks exchange and endorse so-called letters of credit which give rise to a payment if the goods are presented or which allow for the transfer of the goods if proof of payment is presented at the harbour entrepôt.

Depending on the level of trust between trading partners and the actual need for external finance, a number of *modi operandi* can be observed (Table 3.2). Cash on order implies that the bill must be paid before the goods are shipped and thus the risk of this transaction fully rests with the importing company. A letter of credit (or a documentary trade credit) is a bank statement that the importer is able to make the payment; this assurance can even be extended so that it also includes the trustworthiness of the importer's bank (in which case the exporter's bank confirms the letter of credit). This is of course a bit more expensive because of the bank fees involved. The documentary payment collection, likewise, is a bank service to collect the payment and the relevant documents from the importer. The most risky form of payment for the exporter is an open account, where payment takes place only after delivery. Typically, this manner of finance is only available in markets where competition is high (and then it is generally speaking an aspect of a competitive offer) and/or between repeat buyers and sellers that have a long history of transactions which builds trust.

Table 3.2 Major trade finance methods and point in time where risk is transferred from the exporter to the importer

	Date of contract	Transportation		Date of payment after delivery
		Departure	Arrival	
Cash on order (Cash-in-advance)	●			
Letter of credit		●		
Documentary collection			●	
Open account				●

During the 2007 financial crises industry-wide shifts occurred out of risky trade financing (in particular open accounts) and into more secure payments (from the exporter's perspective) and bank intermediated products such as letters of credit and documentary credit (Table 3.3).

Table 3.3 Composition of trade finance business (October 2007–January 2009) in per cent

	October 2007	October 2008	January 2009
Cash in advance	19	20	22
Bank-intermediated	33	35	36
Open account	48	45	42
	100	100	100

Source: International Monetary Fund – Banking Association For Trade, 2009

A financial crisis may especially hit international trade activities. Firstly, banks and banking services are more (and often much more) important for international activities than for domestic activities (see on this issue, for example, Fingerand and Schuknecht, 1999 and Auboin and Meier-Ewert,

2003). Secondly, internationally active firms will need finance over longer periods than firms that only work in and sell on the local market. Of course all firms (also those that are not involved in export or import) need some form of working capital to bridge the time between money outflows (investment in machinery, raw materials, wages, etc.) and the moment that actual payments are received. This working capital is, however, *ceteris paribus* needed for a substantially longer period in international transactions because of the time involved in transportation over much longer distances. Banks are essential in this process as they often provide the working capital to the business firm. Secondly, international payments are much more complicated because of different and variable exchange rates and the involvement of different jurisdictions. Exchange rate volatility is a risk for the exporter and the importer because the amount of local currency that is involved in the transaction is uncertain. The fact that legal systems and legal requirements between countries differ complicates matters even more. It is also difficult for firms to observe the creditworthiness of trade partners that are located in other countries. Banks are important providers of insurance against and knowledge about these risks. Thirdly, and in contrast to domestic trade, payment in cash is not a viable alternative in international transactions so that banks always need to be involved either because they provide cheques, letters of credit or simply electronic payment. So international payment is different from national payment and this is even true in a monetary union (such as EMU) where the currency is common to all trading partners involved.

It is, however, not only the fact that international trade crucially depends on financial services to finance trade-related expenditure and to insure against trade-related risk that makes international trade vulnerable during periods of financial instability. Equally important is that actually payments need to be settled by involving several banks that function under different regulatory supervision regimes so that thrust between the financial institutions involved is a *sine qua non*. During financial crises thrust collapses and thus international exchange is in peril.

It is thus no wonder that many observers have considered insufficient trade finance and trade credit to be a highly likely suspect for the world trade collapse.

4. RECENT EMPIRICAL FINDINGS

An unfortunate consequence of the lack of a consistent data series on trade finance and trade credit is that a longer-term perspective cannot be provided on the development of global trade finance before and during the trade collapse. Trade analysts and policy makers have followed a number of different empirical strategies to cope with this particular problem including the use of surveys (which mainly report perceptions and directions of change at some point in time), the study of proxy variables (in particular related to lending standards and monetary conditions) as well as more detailed studies of observable but indirect variables related to trade credit (actual lending activity in terms of contracts is an example).

The available studies provide a broad picture of the conditions on formal and informal financial markets, but it definitely is a bridge too far to draw strong conclusions for trade finance *per se* from these studies. Firstly, the observations are mainly indirect and assume (but never establish) a relationship between the observable proxy variable and the unobserved variable of interest, that is volume of trade finance. Second, sampling during a crisis has many problems. Typically the sampling has not been done on a random basis and the response appears to have been selective so that some countries with large banks are not surveyed. An example is the April 2009 *Trade Finance Survey* of the International Monetary Fund and the Banking Association For Trade (2009) which covers the period October 2007–January 2009 and the activities of 44 banks located in 23 countries, but does not include a Dutch bank although the Netherlands is in the top ten of trading nations and had three global international banks before the outbreak of the financial crisis.[10] Indeed, a sample bias is to be expected because many financial institutions no longer exist. This implies that the fallacies of composition and hasty generalization may be relevant here. Only survivors can be sampled, of course, and in a shrinking market the survivors can actually report an increase in the outstanding volume of their trade finance, because they will attract some of the business of banks that go bankrupt. The fact that we do not have random samples is further complicated by the problems posed by self-selection. Banks that can make strategic gains by responding will be more likely to participate in surveys. This is particularly relevant since strategic behaviour is characteristic for any environment where regulation and supervision are in a flux. Typically, we therefore do not know the actual amounts of global finance and we do not even know the direction of global finance with any accuracy or confidence. In view of the data deficiencies it is understandable that the analyses on this topic often appear to be contradictory and give rise to different assessments of the need for specific policies.

Financial Tightness

One of the earliest attempts to guesstimate the impact of a reduction in trade finance occurs in the OECD's June 2009 general assessment of the macroeconomic situation (OECD 2009b) where the OECD secretariat reports on an assessment of the role of financial conditions in driving trade. Noting reports of a contracting availability of trade finance, the OECD staff included a proxy for global finance availability in its model of world trade finding an improvement in the fit of the model to recent data, as this accounts for close to a third of the trade collapse in the fourth quarter of 2008 and the first quarter of 2009 (OECD 2009b, p. 23). A further investigation that provides a better understanding of the impact of credit restrictions in the OECD world trade model is Cheung and Guichard (2009). Since the OECD findings are widely quoted and also because they motivated many policy initiatives it pays to see what has actually been done. First of all, the OECD staff is careful to point out that it is 'difficult to quantify the trade finance squeeze in the absence of time series on trade finance' (Cheun and Guichard, 2009, p. 10) and thus proceeds to include three proxies in the world trade model: the net percentage of banks reporting a tightening in credit, the high yield spread on ten year government bonds, and a financial stress variable that basically is an interaction term between credit spread and credit availability. Importantly these variables are all measured in US markets. According to Cheun and Guichard (2009, p. 17):

> This choice is justified by both the strong correlation of bond spreads and the absence of a long history on credit availability surveys outside the United States. Nonetheless, these proxies for trade finance may underestimate the impact on trade if financial crises tend to restrict trade finance relatively more than other forms of credit.

Econometrically the addition of credit standards and financial stress variables appears to be successful: the variables are highly significant and the adjusted-R^2 improves a bit from 0.50 to 0.56. There are, however, on closer inspection quite some problems with the reported findings. In particular the results depend on the proxy that is being used and differ dramatically so that no robust conclusion emerges. Firstly, the magnitude of the effect (and thus its economic policy relevance) is rather small for the credit standards as a 10 per cent balance of firms with tightening credit would reduce world trade in the short run only by less than 1 per cent per annum. Secondly, the reported impact of the financial stress proxy is sizeable as 'it removes about 13 percentage points of world trade growth, explains about 45% of the collapse' (Cheun and Guichard 2009, p. 18). The proxy, however, becomes completely insignificant in specifications that included indicators for the presence of international value chains, in particular a measure of vertical supply integration.[11] Also the third proxy – the spreads variable – was insignificant. Actually, 'when included on its own [it] produced even worse equation fit, and the results are therefore not reported' (*sic*). Cheun and Guichard (2009, pp. 21–2, especially Table 4) also provide an in-depth analysis of the out-of-sample predictions for the trade collapse that were generated by the model on the basis of the available data for the independent variables in 2006Q4, 2007Q4 and 2008Q3. None of the specifications of the model is able to predict the world trade collapse in 2008–2009 completely. Most forecasting errors in per cent of the total decline in trade are in the range of 40 per cent and higher. One particularly strange and counterintuitive finding is that the forecasting errors of the model increase when the forecasting horizon decreases (see Figure 3.3 which illustrates the normal pattern of decreasing forecast errors for shorter forecasting horizons for the naive model and the abnormal findings for the other specifications of the OECD's world trade equation). This seems to imply that 'incorporating information on activity in the most recent quarters actually worsened the forecast accuracy [for the world trade collapse]' (Cheun and Guichard 2009, p. 21). One interpretation would be that trade growth did not (or did to a significantly decreasing degree) respond to the main theoretical drivers identified by the OECD. In particular the tightening of credit conditions does not appear to have had the expected negative impact on world trade growth.[12]

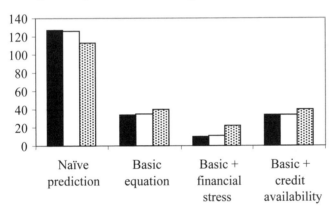

■ 2006Q4 □ 2007Q4 ▣ 2008Q3

Note: The naïve prediction relates to an AR(*q*) benchmark equation. The basis equation
          relates world trade to world GDP. The two other equations include in addition a
          financial stress variable and a credit availability measure respectively
Source: Cheung and Guichard (2009), Table 4, p. 22

*Figure 3.3   Forecast errors for the trade collapse in 2008Q4 of the OECD
              world trade equation for different forecasting horizons (in per
              cent)*

All in all the OECD secretariat produced an equation that showed an economically meaningful impact of financial distress on trade only in the specification that was most likely to suffer from omitted variable bias (due to the exclusion of a vertical integration variable) while the other specifications of the world trade model and the other considered proxies showed small and generally insignificant coefficients only.

Trade Credit

The leading empirical study on the relationship between trade credit and the evolution of trade around the year 2008 undoubtedly is the study by Levchenko et al. (2009) which provides a detailed cross-section analysis for the US at the sector level.[13] The study investigates which factors determine the reduction of bilateral trade flows between June 2008 and June 2009. A strength of this study is that it is not only concerned with exports, but also takes the collapse of US imports into account.

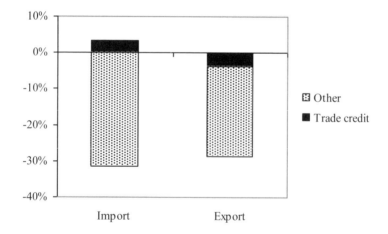

Source: Levchenko et al. (2009), Table 11, p. 36

Figure 3.4 Contribution of trade finance to aggregate reduction in US trade

The paper by Levchenko et al. evaluates the trade collapse against the recent history of trade fluctuations and finds that is exceptional in nature compared to this benchmark. It, moreover, attempts to evaluate these developments analysing the impact of three sets of variables that test three different hypotheses for the trade collapse: the occurrence of international value chains (vertical production linkages), compositional differences in demand (both by sector and final demand category) and variations in the level of trade credit.[14] The latter is measured by two standard indicators: the ratio of accounts payable to costs of the sold goods and the ratio of accounts receivable to sales. Using Compustat data Levchenko et al. (2009) find no evidence at the firm level that either exports or imports were reduced more strongly in sectors where trade credit is relatively important. They observe a contraction of trade credit at the firm level but median accounts receivable and payable are only 1–2 per cent lower than the peak level of 2007. So the reduction in trade credit in the US actually appears to have been quite small during the period of the trade collapse. Trade credit is only significant in the regressions for manufacturing imports.

Detailed simulations illustrate that the trade credit effect can produce a 3.8 percentage points reduction for exports (where the total observed reduction is 29 percentage points), but the reported impact on imports is actually a counterintuitive increase (see Figure 3.4). All in all the trade credit effect appears to account for 12.5 per cent of the trade collapse, a result that is more or less in line with the earlier discussed results for financial tightness.

Trade Finance

In order to solve the data paucity the international organizations (co) organized surveys of private and public parties involved in trade finance both as a creditor and as a debtor. A useful survey of recent surveys is Mora and Powers (2009). Typically these studies find (i) a broadly based decline of cross-border finance from all sources, (ii) a change in the composition of trade finance due to less risk appetite of exporters (that is a shift of risk from exporters to importers and an increasing use of banks and official export insurers) and (iii) a consensus view that trade finance had been the number two contributor to the global export collapse (the number one cause is falling global effective demand). In addition the findings in the surveys were used as an argument in the debate as it provided a sense of urgency to proposed policy initiatives.

Not all surveys are in the public domain so that we often have to rely on secondary sources and indirect quotations. This could be worrisome since the butcher so to say has to check the meat that he is selling: the staff of the international organizations provides the interpretation of these surveys and – like their fellow economists – appear to have been a bit prejudiced in the interpretation of the survey results. This is of course not always the case – Dorsey (2009) and Mora and Powers (2009) are examples of reasonably balanced reports – but many people in the trade finance industry saw a trade finance collapse, because they were led to believe that the trade finance collapse caused the trade collapse. But did it? Or does causality run in the other direction? Obviously this is a crucial issue with potentially quite disturbing implications for recent policy initiatives.

Let us consider one of the leading surveys in somewhat more detail. The widely quoted April 2009 *Trade Finance Survey* of the International Monetary Fund and the Banking Association For Trade (2009) showed only a substantial decrease in the value of letters of credit and actually pointed out that little noticeable change had occurred in the percentage of banks reporting a change in other trade finance product lines (such as Export Credit Insurance and Short-term Export Working Capital). More importantly there appears to be an issue of causality: did world trade collapse because of lacking finance or did trade finance collapse because of lacking international trade? Interestingly 73 per cent of the responding banks mentioned a decline of trade activities as the most important reason for the decline in trade finance. The *Trade Finance Survey* is, however, all too often quoted for the finding that the trade finance was the number two cause for the trade collapse (57 per cent of the respondents pointed out less credit availability at their own institution and less credit availability at their counterparty banks as a major cause).[15] So the response actually provided quite strong a case for the hypothesis that the trade collapse was driving the developments in the volume of trade finance. Interestingly, it was observed that the majority view was that 'lower credit availability contributed to declining trade earlier in the crisis, but this share fell in later surveys' (Mora and Powers 2009, p. 121). Typically, one would expect such a pattern of changing perceptions if the starting point is a very strong professional *a priori* conviction on a cause that is falsified over time so that learning takes place and respondents change their views accordingly. As such the surveys have probably not told the story that many observers appear to have read in them.

Dissatisfaction with surveys which only provide snapshots at certain points in time may have been the motivation to construct time series from which the development of trade finance could be gleaned. By early 2010 several data series were being reconstructed that could provide a rough picture of the developments of trade finance. Often these reconstructions provided intelligent new proxies for the intensity by which trade financed was accessed. A nice example is Chauffour et al. (2010, p. 4, Figure 1) who use the number of trade messages exchanged through the Society for Worldwide Interbank Financial Telecommunication (SWIFT). This is a relevant indicator of trade finance activity since international banks will have to communicate with each other about the conditions and financial arrangements related to letters of credit, payments, etc. Interestingly, the significant decrease in the number of messages by some −15 per cent *vis-à-vis* the same period in the previous year occurs in the first months of 2009, almost a quarter after the onset of the world trade collapse.

Figure 3.5 illustrates this point combining growth rates for world trade and global finance data derived from a slightly different set of SWIFT data.[16] Clearly trade leads finance: trade finance activity is still increasing when the trade collapse sets in and also the much larger reduction in the volume of trade suggests that trade finance in all likelihood has not been the driver of the trade collapse. Of course the figure does not prove this point as it is based on indirect observation for trade finance activities, but it is a strong indication.

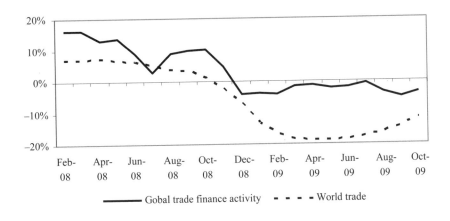

Notes: World trade: 3 months centred moving average of real growth rate of world trade *vis-à-vis* same month in previous year.

                 Global trade finance activity: 3 months moving average of growth rate of number of messages exchanged in SWIFT system *vis-à-vis* same month in previous year

Sources: Word trade: *CPB World Trade Monitor*. Global finance activity: www.swift.com

Figure 3.5   *Growth rates of world trade and global trade finance activity,
2008–2009*

All in all the story that emerges from the newly discovered and constructed data series does not provide convincing support for the mainstream analysis, explanation and/or narrative for the movements of trade finance in 2008–2009. The data do suggest a relative increase in the incentives to insure trade especially in the segment of medium- to long-term commitments. The demand appears to have been met by official export credit agencies rather than by banks and private insurers thus reflecting what some consider to be one of the successes of the trade finance policy initiatives.

But is it a success? The data suggest an alternative story. The world trade collapse depressed the market for trade finance. Substitution of private and public credit would then occur due to abundant supply of public credit (which typically has a longer maturity) that crowded out short-term finance (which typically is supplied by the private sector). If the alternative provides the true picture, public money has been wasted and the banks have been deprived of a relatively riskless international activity. This of course begs the questions if and why such a policy error could have occurred.

5. POLICY INITIATIVES

Trade finance was actually on the policy agenda long before the trade collapse occurred. Partly this was a consequence of developments during the Asia crisis which led to a network of policy analysts and policy makers related to the Working Group on Trade, Development and Finance. One particularly relevant project was the Aid-for-Trade Initiative that aimed at reducing barriers to the integration of developing countries in the world economy. The Initiative in particular dealt with the shortage of trade finance and the lack of guarantee infrastructures for developing countries. Policy makers at the international institutions were therefore well prepared to analyse and discuss financial packages and arrangements that could cope with a trade finance collapse in the wake of a financial crisis.

Surveys during the early phase of the world trade collapse provided estimates for the deficiency of trade finance ranging from $25 billion to $500 billion (Chauffour and Farole 2009). According to Auboin (2009b, p. 10) estimates were converging to a market gap in the order of magnitude of a few hundred billion US dollars. This 'gap' provided a stimulus for policy proposals to restore the availability of trade finance but with little or no reflection on the justification of government intervention (see, however, Chauffour and Farole 2009 for a critical review). The April 2009 meeting of the G20 took action and announced additional trade financing of $250 billion, including instruments to mitigate risks and liquidity support. According to the G20 Trade Finance Expert Group (2009, p. 1) by August 2009, an increase of the G20 members involved in the trade finance initiative from 12 to 16 countries had even increased the potential support available to $400 billion.

Part of the support package was, however, pure window dressing (using existing capacity that simply had not been used prior to the G20 initiative and headroom) and moreover the trade finance initiative seems to have overshot the amount actually required by the market. It was therefore no surprise that the G20 Trade Finance Expert Group (2009, p. 3) concluded that 'banks and buyers have utilised on aggregate approximately 63 per cent of the G20's commitment capacity in the first six months'. Note that it is, moreover, quite possible that crowding out of private trade finance by official export credit agencies pushed up that percentage substantially.

It is, on a final note, not uncommon that estimates for public funds grossly exaggerate the actual capital requirements and/or absorption capacity of involved parties. In the early 1990s completely unrealistic estimates circulated, for example, for the external funds needed to finance the transition in Eastern Europe (van Bergeijk and Lensink 1993). There is a resemblance between this debate in the 1990s and the trade finance debate and that is the relative neglect of the importance of open borders to stimulate trade. Admittedly, the G20 pleaded strongly against protectionism. But these were words that could not mask policy inaction as the Doha Round of WTO multilateral trade negotiations was not brought to a conclusion. The G20 trade finance initiative may actually have served as the figleaf to hide this inaction.

NOTES

[1] On a historical note: also in the 1930s a collapse of trade finance occurred, see Kindleberger (1978), p. 72.

[2] IMF (2003) offers an overview of lessons drawn from the Asia crisis and their potential implications for the DotCom crisis around the start of the millennium.

[3] See Kindleberger (1973) and Rothermund (1996) on the impact of the financial crisis of the 1930s on the informal capital markets in the periphery.

[4] The OECD (2010) notes that 'Overall, these figures result in additional aid of USD 27 billion from 2004 to 2010, but a USD 21 billion shortfall between what donors promised in 2005 and the OECD estimates for the 2010 outcome.' So rather than letting the automatic stabilizers do their work, the wealthy countries appear to inject automatic destabilization into these economies.

[5] For the first quarter of 2009 UNCTAD (2009a) estimates a decrease by 54 per cent on the basis of a broader sample of the 57 countries for which quarterly data on FDI inflows are available

[6] See, for example Bergstrand and Egger (2010) on the relationship between FDI and trade in final goods and intermediate goods

[7] Note that Chapter 4, Section 2, discusses some statistical issues related to the measurement of trade that may also have an impact on this relationship.

[8] See Auboin (2009b, p. 11) for a discussion on some statistical issues regarding the trade finance series.

[9] Some theoretical explanations for the occurrence of intra-firm credit may not be related to the occurrence of trade collapses and/or finance squeezes although they may have substantial explanatory power regarding the questions of why vendors and buyers provide credit to their trading partners. These explanations include theories that explain non-financial credits on the basis of quality guarantees, price

discrimination and as an element of non-price competition or non-observable discounts (that are discounts that are not reflected in official price lists).

[10] The survey covered Australia, Canada, Chile, Denmark, France, Germany, Greece, Ireland, Italy, Kazakhstan, Mexico, New Zealand, Norway, Portugal, Romania, Russia, Spain, Saudi Arabia, Switzerland, Turkey, the UK, Uruguay and the USA.

[11] See Cheung and Guichard (2009, Table 2, p. 18, column 5 and Table A4, p. 31, column 5). Incidentally, the same problem occurs with the credit standards proxy, see Cheun and Guichard (Table 3, p. 20, column 2 and Table A5, p.32, specification 7). We will return to the interpretation of these finding in Chapter 4 when we discuss the international value chain hypothesis.

[12] Van Leeuwe (2009) has examined the relationship between credit restrictions and trade by focusing on the impact of financial tightness on inventories which may be an important driver of import demand. Analysing US import volume over the period 1991Q1–2005Q2 van Leeuwe (2009) does not find a statistically significant effect although he argues that it is economically meaningful.

[13] Other studies that deal with periods before the world trade collapse find a more significant impact, see for example Awati and Weinstein (2009) on Japan. It is, however, not straightforward that their findings could be generalized for the world trade collapse.

[14] Chapter 4 discusses their findings with regard to international value chains.

[15] An example is Mora and Powers (2009), p. 121.

[16] This analysis uses the data for regional numbers of messages which are in the public domain on www.swift.com since the start of 2007 on a year-to-date basis.

4. The International Value Chain Myth

When the extent of the trade collapse became clear many observers were keen to relate the speed and significance of the reduction in global trade flows to the fact that products were produced in global value chains with different parts of the production process allocated to different countries. As pointed out by Escaith (2009, p. 1) the trade collapse changed the perspective of the public and the policy makers on international value chains dramatically:

> International supply chains, one of the most salient features of the 'new globalization', were rapidly identified as one of the main factors for [the] synchronization of shocks. With unemployment increasing as recession spread in developed countries, the debate was also put on the public place as the delocalization of investment and jobs that rests behind these new productive networks (…) became the focus of much public scrutiny (Escaith, 2009, p. 1).

Many professional economists agreed. The intuition was that the international division of labour had changed dramatically. This change was in particular due to the fragmentation that is inherent to globalization processes: products are no longer produced in one country to be exported to the rest of the world, but are constructed using intermediate products and services from many countries. It was argued that this explained why the collapse of trade was both quicker and stronger than it had been in the inter bellum. The argumentation for this particular hypothesis was, first of all, that international value chains would spread the reduction of demand to a great many countries at the same time and, secondly, that trade declines would be stronger in international value chains. The first part of the argumentation would seem to fairly reflect a consensus view amongst professional trade analysts who (as we saw in Chapters 1 and 2) stressed the simultaneity of the trade shock at the end of 2008 and the beginning of 2009. Di Giovanni and Levchenko (2009) find that about a third of the co-movement in production between countries may be related to trade in intermediate inputs. Factories in one country depend on factories in other countries and *vice versa*. A shock to a factory thus has an external effect significantly reducing the output of its trading partner (and thus on its host country). Bems et al. (2010) provide a detailed bilateral input–output accounting framework of direct trading relationships between sectors in 55 countries and regions (*inter alia* abstracting from changes that work via macroeconomic demand) which explains about three fifths of the fall in world trade. The second element of the argumentation relates to the magnifying effect of developments in the value chain. This may reflect the fact that a reduction in the availability of intermediate inputs can become a serious bottleneck in an economy (Escaith 2009) or it may be the consequence of the fact that trade is not measured properly (and often double-counted) *vis-à-vis* production (and its aggregate GDP). As both the share of intermediate inputs and the elasticity of world trade to GDP increased significantly over recent decades observers such as Freund (2009a and b) and Cheung and Guichard (2009) have assumed a causal relationship between the two (the point is not that there is a correlation; the point is that this is assumed to be a one-directional causal relationship).

All in all it seemed that the existence of a network of international value chains could explain both the propagation of shocks (and thus the simultaneity of the trade collapse in many countries) and the severity of the trade shock (the fact that the percentage reduction of trade was a manifold of the percentage reduction in GDP).

Most economists would also seem to agree that – due to the increased openness of most economies and the increasingly numerous global linkages between businesses – the transmission of the reduction in effective demand had changed. The decline in import demand that was a consequence of the financial crisis was thus assumed to have been stronger than in earlier periods when trade was more specialized than today as its character was more inter-industry than intra-industry. The first trade pattern characterization (inter-industry) is used when exports and imports consist of completely different products (such as when a country is exporting oil and importing food); the second manner of trade pattern is characterized by imports and exports that consist of the same products (a country for example both exports and imports car components).

The profession's apparent agreement, however, on the stylized fact that the trade transmission mechanism was probably stronger and quicker in the recent trade collapse than in, for example, the 1930s does not imply that international value chains were causing the strength and speed of the trade collapse (and it surely does not imply that all economists were sharing this view). Many argue that the share of value chains in trade has increased a lot (but note that many measurement issues are relevant in this field; see Box 4.1). Since this trend in the extent of intermediate goods trade has, however, been associated with an increase in globalization, the hypothesis that international value chain activities provide a counterbalancing force against deglobalization would *a priori* seem to be equally valid from a logical point of view. These two contrasting views on the impact and implications of international value chains constitute the central theme of this chapter.

Box 4.1 Data on value chain activity

The empirical analysis of theories related to value chain activities is hampered by a lack of statistics.[*] We do not have systematic information about the composition and location of components in international value chains because these are corporate secrets and because the trade registration system does not account for it. In order to glean this phenomenon much economic detective work is required and many data sources have been used creatively to deduce valuable grains of evidence. Amador and Cabral (2009) provide an overview of studies and the (relative) merits of methods that have been applied to this issue:

- *Custom statistics* provide insights into the locally (domestically) value added component of international composites if the tax laws provide for exemption or different tariff rates for the domestic import component of imported goods.
- *Trade statistics* are used to identify goods that are expected to be intermediate inputs (typically these would be classified in the standard trade classification SITC as machinery and equipment (SITC7) or miscellaneous manufactured goods (SITC 8)).
- *Input–output tables* describing business-to-business trade at the aggregate level of sectors can be used to calculate imported input shares in production, imports and exports.

Different data sources require different methodologies and tell different stories. The share of value chains has increased a lot and, for example, vertical specialization may account for almost one quarter of international trade flows (according to estimates by Miroudot and Ragoussis 2009).[**] Others, such as for example, Bergstrand and Egger (2010) find that the share of intra-firm trade has remained rather stable, that the patterns of trade in final goods and trade in intermediates are strikingly similar and that intermediate goods trade amongst OECD countries was slower than the rate of growth registered for final goods (but the reverse can be observed for South–South and South–North trade). All in all it is important to realize that no accurate, unambiguous statistical measure exists.

[*] This is also true at a more general level for other variables (so beyond the trade statistics issue) as noted by Peels et al. (2009, p. 4): 'In late 2008 and early 2009 there was no reliable public information available on inventories and sales across different echelons of the supply chain'.

[**] This is the trade-weighed number. The literature often quotes the simple un-weighted average over countries of about one third.

Section 1 introduces the concept of international value chains and reviews
the literature that deals with the simultaneous increasing trends in the share of
international value chains in total trade and the ratio of world trade to world
GDP that both accelerated around 1995. Section 2 focuses on some of the
measurement issues that many have suggested as the explanation par
excellence for this simultaneity. Section 3 deals with the available empirical
evidence on the speed of transmission in international value chains during the
trade collapse and its relationship with shares of manufacturing trade (exports
and imports), intra-industry trade and vertical specialization. Section 4 draws
some conclusions

1. INTERNATIONAL VALUE CHAINS AND GLOBALIZATION

The value chain argument has a strong intuitive and empirical appeal because
many modern products are international composites which means that the
production process has been fragmented. Components are built in those
locations that have a comparative or competitive advantage for a particular
part of the production process. This fragmentation of the international value
chain is efficient as companies produce in those countries where production
costs are lowest. Also other organizational components of the value chain
(design, assembly, marketing, finance, and so on) are often in principle
geographically mobile so that tasks rather than concrete products can be
outsourced as well. The latter process is highly relevant for the world
economy although its impact on the collapse of trade is quite uncertain
(typically trade in services has suffered less during trade collapses).[1] Anyhow,
the international fragmentation of the production process has been seen both
as a driver of globalization – especially since the mid 1990s – and as one of
the key reasons for the speed and strength of the world trade collapse. It is
thus interesting to take a closer look at the working of such an international
value chain.

   Consider the international value chain of Apple's iPod that has been charted
by Linden et al. (2007). Table 4.1 summarizes the available information on
the international network of firms involved in the production of this product.
Gathering this manner of information for concrete products incidentally often
requires a lot of economic detective work because the components, prices and
suppliers are considered to be business secrets. With this caveat in mind we
can note that the hard drive is supplied by Toshiba, but produced in China,
the display by Toshiba-Matsushita and produced in Japan and the video
processor is supplied by Broadcom but produced in Singapore or Taiwan.
These complex products themselves often have multinational supply lines,

involving locations in many countries that are not reported in Table 4.1 and, moreover, many less important components are also produced all around the world. Apple organizes the international value chain providing market knowledge, intellectual property, system integration and cost management skills, and a brand name (note that Apple's activities create more than half the value added). China inserts, tests and assembles these components. Indeed, if we buy an iPod we use knowledge, labour and capital from all around the world.

Table 4.1 Value chain of iPod (5th generation, October 2003)

	Firm	HQ	Location	Costs ($)	Per cent of costs	Un-allocated
Harddrive	Toshiba	Japan	China	73.39	25	53.94
Display	Toshiba	Japan	Japan	20.39	7	14.54
Videoprocessor	Broadway	US	Singapore	8.36	3	3.97
Other components				42.26	14	38.58
Direct costs				*144.40*	*48*	*111.03*
Apple				80	27	
Retail				45	15	
Distribution				30	10	
Consumer price				299.40	100	

Note: HQ is location of headquarters
Source: Linden et al. (2007)

The upshot is clear. If consumers reduce their demand for iPods (or for any other international composite for that matter) firms in many countries around the globe will be experiencing declines in their sales volumes.

Not a New Phenomenon

This fragmentation of international value chains is by no means a recent phenomenon. Porter (1990) and Reich (1991), for example, at the start of the 1990s already pointed out that modern consumption and production patterns increasingly were characterized by internationally traded goods as well as 'domestic' goods which increasingly contained substantial foreign inputs, and that international exchange therefore more and more pertained to intangibles such as research, marketing and advertising as well as routine components and service. So while this process was not something new in the third millennium, attention was focussed again on the international fragmentation of production due to the speed with which trade increased, especially in comparison to the rate of growth of world production. Figure 1.5 illustrates the acceleration of the rising trend in the trade-to-GDP ratio, especially since 1995. The increase in the elasticity of trade with respect to income has been explicitly linked to associated with the development of vertical specialization in trade and supply integration (see, for example Cheung and Guichard 2009, pp. 14–16). Table 4.2 shows that whereas the relationship between vertical supply integration and the trade-to-GDP ratio was quite stable in the period 1990–99, it showed considerable fluctuations after that period. In the early 2000s openness actually increased at a higher rate than vertical supply integration in the world; after 2004 we see the opposite pattern. Notably, Amador and Cabral (2009, Figure 1, p. 275) show declines over the period 1967–2005 at some levels of aggregation and since the turn of the century for all levels of aggregation.

Table 4.2 Ratio of world vertical supply integration to openness (index numbers 1990=100, 1990–2005)

Period average 1990–94	90.4
Period average 1995–99	89.1
2000	80.0
2001	63.3
2002	81.5
2003	83.3
2004	111.8
2005	121.6

Source: Calculations based on Amador and Cabral (2009)

The relationship between openness and fragmentation appears to have been quite unstable.[2] Possible explanations include changes in relative prices of intermediate goods[3] and of course and obviously the possibility that 'total world imports are increasing for reasons other than V[ertical]S[pecialization] activities', as rightly pointed out by Amador and Cabral (2009, p. 275). The economic profession, however, for better or worse seems to have by and large accepted the argument that international value chain activity has a multiplier effect on trade flows.

Value Chains as Transmission Mechanism

An implication of the value chain narrative is that the trade flows of many countries involved in the internationally fragmented production process will be influenced if demand for such an international composite is hit. The financial crisis thus spreads much wider and much quicker through the trade channel than in earlier times when trade was more concentrated in final goods.

Indeed, international value chains often seem to act as the central neural system of the world economy transmitting economic information between upstream and downstream producers that are located all around the world through market processes.[4] Typically, upstream firms will expect that all downstream firms will react in the same manner (for example by de-stocking) so that sales variance that is measured upstream will tend to exceed downstream variance. In their analysis of developments in supply chains in the years 2008 and 2009 Peels et al. (2009), moreover, show that business-to-business markets contract in general quicker than consumer markets. Likewise, fluctuations in manufacturing will exceed those in retail.

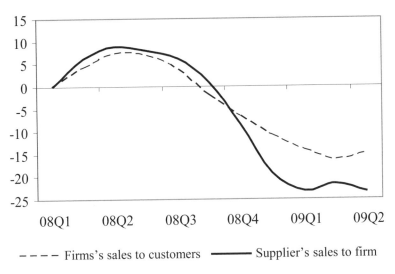

– – – – Firms's sales to customers	——— Supplier's sales to firm

Source: Unweighted simple average based on publicly reported data from DSM, Philips, Akzo Nobel and Thyssen Krupp (Peels et al., 2009, p. 6 and appendix)

Figure 4.1   Bullwhip effect 2008Q1–2009Q2 (per cent deviation from levels at the start of 2008Q1)

Figure 4.1 illustrates the bullwhip effect by which the financial crisis hit the average sales of four multinationals and their suppliers. The figure also shows the much stronger reduction on average of supplier sales to these four firms in comparison to their own sales suggesting that de-stocking must have been substantial.[5] All in all, Figure 4.1, which is based on publicly reported data by key multinationals, offers a very vivid visual illustration of how (Peels et al. 2009, p. 4) 'a single pulse by a synchronized decrease in the target inventory level along the entire supply chain' works out.

These stylized facts are in line with the key hypotheses of the narrative that points to global value chains as one of the key determinants of the speed and strength of the trade collapse in 2008–2009. This value chain argument provides two testable hypotheses, namely that trade in manufactured goods is especially vulnerable during trade collapses and that internationally trading firms (which are upstream firms) will experience stronger fluctuations in sales than the changes in final demand registered by downstream retail firms which are directly confronted with consumer demand fluctuations.

Note, however, that this analysis is of a partial nature only and that it is based on a biased sample, namely only of those companies that are *involved* in international value chains. It would simply be logically wrong to conclude from the studies that were discussed in the present section that the value chain caused the extraordinarily depth and duration of the 2008–2009 trade collapse. That conclusion would require a sample that also includes international firms *not involved* in value chains. This is so because we need to consider, firstly, that such firms may show stronger or weaker declines in their sales, but also because firms may change their behaviour and substitute away from value chain activities (that is reduce the fragmentation of the chain). This reminds us again that moving from findings at the micro (firm) level to the macroeconomic level entails the risks of the fallacy of composition and the micro–macro paradox.

2. INTERNATIONAL VALUE CHAINS AND THE MEASUREMENT OF WORLD TRADE

Yet another factor is often mentioned in relation to international value chains. The fragmentation of the production process would seem to imply that more trade will occur for the same product. Intermediate products and components may cross many borders before they end up in the final product. It has been observed that components sometimes cross the same border multiple times. And each time a component or intermediate product crosses a border it is 'double' counted as international trade. Thus fragmentation would increase international trade even if the underlying final demand does not change.

This measurement issue deserves close scrutiny. It actually appears very obvious at first sight, but the 'apparent and intuitive truth' of this idea is no guarantee that it offers an accurate understanding of reality. Interestingly, recent studies that develop an accounting framework that takes fragmentation and international forward and backward linkages seriously, derive completely opposite conclusions. Bénassy-Quéré et al. (2009, p. 11) conclude that 'fragmented supply chains are consistent with world trade reacting *proportionally* to a fall in world GDP' (so that the elasticity is 1); Bems et al. (2010) derive a global trade elasticity with respect to output of 2.3. It is remarkable that *accounting* frameworks can produce such different results. The explanation is most likely that the international trade registration system does not provide systematic information about the composition and location of components in international value chains so that many critical assumptions need to be made even in the application of basic accounting for trade. These assumptions may actually drive the results.

Anyhow, the idea that fragmentation inflates measured international trade continues to be a key issue in discussions about the trade collapse also because this concept claims to offer an explanation for two phenomena at the same time: the increase in the trade-to-GDP ratio before and the strength of downturn during the trade collapse. So let us take a closer look at how measurement of trade and fragmentation of production, vertical specialization and decisions on the location of economic activity are related.

Non-problematic Trade Flows

The first point to note is that fragmentation of the production process, in contrast to what is often assumed, does not by definition imply that trade is being double counted. Fragmentation only provides a problem if the total trade flow is influenced and this is not always the case. Such fragmentation of international supply chains is non-problematic. It does not 'blow-up' trade and it is also not associated with the strength of the trade collapse. Consider, for example, Figure 4.2 that illustrates a hypothetical case where inputs for the production of a good were originally imported from country A at a value of 100 (top panel). The bottom panel shows that country B can increase its supplier base and outsource to more countries without an increase in measured global trade. Country B now imports 20 from country A and 80 from country C with no impact on total trade that still has a value of 100. But the value chain has become more international by any standard as more countries are now involved in the supply chain. The measurement distortion of international trade will also not occur when a firm sets up a production facility to serve as an export platform to other countries. The increase in trade that results from such investments is genuine. Many more instances exist where fragmentation of the international value chain does not 'distort' trade figures.

a   Traditional non-fragmented trade flow from country A to B (global trade
     is 100)

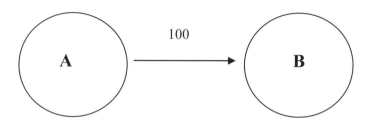

b   Fragmented trade flow without measurement problem from countries A
     and C to B (global trade is 100)

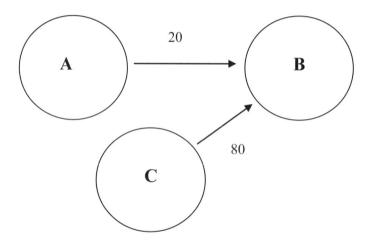

Figure 4.2   Examples of non-problematic trade flows

Problematic Trade Flows

This is not to deny, however, that the statistical issue can of course have a
merit in many cases where the production process is fragmented. Figure 4.3
illustrates two such cases. The top panel illustrates what happens if country B
exports intermediate goods or raw materials with a value of 20 to country A
for further processing and later imports final products (or products at a more
final stage of production) with a value of 100 that use these intermediate
goods or raw materials. While value added in country B is only 80, total trade

is now measured as 120. Likewise, the bottom panel of Figure 4.3 illustrates how total trade can exceed the final value of 100 as country C imports 20 from country A to be processed and exported to country B for a value of 100. In these cases flows in trade may grow (shrink) more strongly than final demand.

a   Country B exports input to county A. Country A exports final product to country B (global trade is 120)

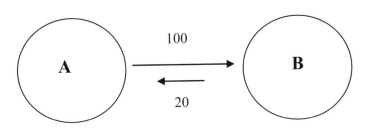

b   Country A exports input to country C. Country C exports final product to country B (global trade is 120)

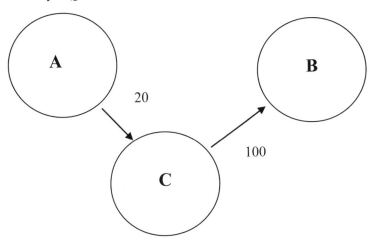

Figure 4.3 Examples of potentially problematic trade flows

It should be noted, however, that an increase in vertical specialization and fragmentation of production processes may also deflate trade figures. Consider, for example, the following simplified case. Country B used to import a product at value 100 from an industry located in country A. If the exporting firm decides to locate a production facility in country B and only exports intermediate products to A (for example, at a value of 20), then trade will actually shrink by 80 because of this foreign direct investment decision. Since the fragmentation of the value chain was increased due to this foreign investment decision, a measure such as the Vertical Specialization Index will increase but at the same time international trade is reduced. This is by no means a theoretical example as this kind of effect could be expected when foreign direct investment is motivated by the desire to be closer to specific markets which in turn can be driven by all kinds of strategic motivations, by transportation cost considerations or by trade barriers.

Some Implications

The clear implication of these examples is that the often assumed relationship (that is: the elasticity) between, on the one hand, fragmentation of international value chains and vertical specialization, and, on the other hand, the speed of globalization (often measured by the ratio of world trade to world production) is not as unambiguous and straightforward as suggested by the recent literature.[6] O'Rourke (2009) makes the same point where he argues that this would require that marginal trade consists of relatively much vertically disintegrated production. If not, the argument may actually work out in the opposite direction.

Still the correlation between international value chain activity and globalization may also be genuine but require a different interpretation as we can speculate that this finding means that globalization is a firm-driven process. Admittedly, the available evidence is suggestive that this process has been associated with an increase in the world's trade-to-GDP ratio, but the mechanism may be quite different from the purely mechanical statistical relationship that relates to the different modes of measurement regarding GDP (value added) and trade (turnover). Value chain interaction may breed trust amongst participating firms because of the repeated-buy character of the transactions and/or have external effects (such as demonstration effects, learning effects or network effects) which support globalization. If this is the case, there is no reason why this role should be asymmetrical (positive in upswings and negative in downturns) as assumed by the dominant narrative.

This has important implications both for the analysis of the world trade collapse and policy advice to stabilize international exchange. The purely mechanical reasoning implies that a collapse can be strong, but that the rebound will be equally strong. One policy implication would seem to be that fragmentation of international value chains increases the fragility and instability of international exchange (and this may induce governments to attempt to become less dependent on intermediate products imported from other countries). Another policy implication could be that no special worries are in order since the process will assure a quick return to the status quo ante. Tanaka (2009) for example notes that 'The good news is that once OECD countries start to recover, the amplification should work in reverse'. The problem with this narrative should by now be clear: it is simply equally logical that international value chains offered support for internationalization, not only before but also during a crisis.[7] If so, policies aimed at reducing the extent to which firms organize themselves in international networks will be very counterproductive. In the economic context of simultaneously increasing globalization, internationalization and vertical specialization an attempt to test these different theoretical visions was probably futile as everything moved in the same direction. But the world trade collapse provides a unique opportunity to see which theory offers the better, more accurate description of the underlying real world processes. We can learn a lot from closer observation of international value chains and the downward movement in the volume of trade, and this is the topic of the next section.

3. DID INTERNATIONAL VALUE CHAINS CAUSE THE STRENGTH OF THE RECENT TRADE COLLAPSE?

Many empirical studies that analyse the relationship between value chain activity on the one hand and world trade and/or openness on the other hand steer clear of the period of trade collapse. A point in case is the report on the OECD world trade model by Cheung and Guischard (2009). They uncover a significant influence on trade – although the elasticity is quantitatively rather small (less than 0.1) – since 1975, but they end their sample just before the crisis breaks out in 2008 because 'this avoids to estimate how VSI evolved during the crisis and make any assumption on the possible distortion to supply chains' (Cheung and Guischard 2009, p. 15) and ... leaves the question in which we are interested completely out. This obviously is a very unsatisfactory situation and several attempts have been done to solve the problem of data paucity. These approaches include partial analyses, single country analyses and calibrated simulation models. The advantages of these approaches are that requirements regarding the number and quality of necessary data (series) are more easily met. The costs are of course that the analysis is less general and/or cannot be generalized in a straightforward manner to other countries and situations.

Partial Analyses

Sometimes analysts are satisfied with pointing out one or two strong cases where the extent of the trade collapse and the share of vertical integration differ markedly and are actually willing to draw conclusions on the bases of two observations. Tanaka (2009) for example argues that

> the difference in vertical FDI strategies between US and Japanese firms is one possible cause of the disproportionally large collapse of trade to global demand contraction. As Japanese firms have embraced vertical FDI, Japan has been more fully immersed in vertical specialization patterns than the US.

It is dangerous of course to deduce a cause from two observations. Figure 4.4 by way of illustration plots the share of vertical specialization in trade against the reduction of the volume of imports for the group of countries that we studied in Chapter 2 (Figure 2.9).[8] There is no apparent relationship between the two suggesting that Tanaka's hypothesis breaks down when the sample is increased beyond his two-country example.

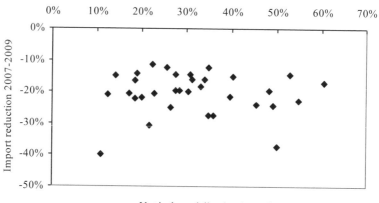

Vertical specialization in trade

Sources: See Figure 2.9 for the import volume reduction. For vertical specialization in trade: OECD 2009d, Table 1

*Figure 4.4   Import reduction during the trade collapse versus share of
         vertical specialization in trade*

In a recent study van Marrewijk (2009) has uncovered similar patterns using the Grubel-Lloyd index for intra-industry trade.[9] Van Marrewijk studies both exports and imports and uses a different sample of countries (he uses another data set than this book derived from the CPB world trade monitor's data set which allows him to study 29 countries that cover more than 86 per cent of world trade[10]). Van Marrewijk does not only analyse the depth as in Figure 4.4 but also studies the duration of the trade collapse as well and the inclination (steepness) of the curve from peak to trough (see Figure 4.5). In addition he uses four different ways to define peak and trough, namely the original raw data, a 5-month centred average, and deviations from trend based on either of these two series. In no case does van Marrewijk find the hypothesized positive correlation between on the one hand, the share of intra-industry trade and on the other hand, the depth, duration and inclination of export and/or import trade declines.

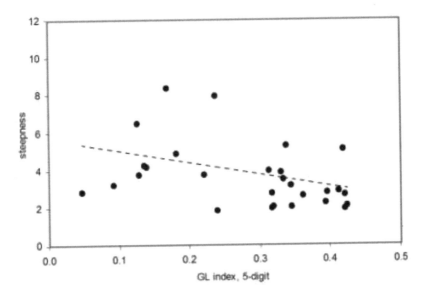

Note: Based on exports that are measured in deviation from their trend

Source: Van Marrewijk (2009)

Figure 4.5   Steepness of the trade collapse and intra-industry trade

On the contrary, van Marrewijk finds negative correlations that often are significant at the usual confidence levels. A little bit more than half the coefficients for intra-industry trade are negative and significant at the usual confidence level of 90 per cent and better in his equations for the decline and steepness of the trade collapse. His empirical evidence thus suggests the existence of a counteracting force. Van Marrewijk speculates that this may actually be due to the fact that the negative impact of a reduction in effective demand is spread across many countries. A fall of intra-industry trade would hurt a country's trade flows one-to-one, but a fall in a fragmented value chain would be smaller for this country since all countries that provide components of the international composite 'share' the burden. Although van Marrewijk sees scope for further research, in particular involving the use of control variables that take other potentially relevant explanatory variables into consideration, he is confident that such extensions of the analysis will not change his basic conclusion that there is no relationship between supply chains and trade contraction.

There would thus seem to exist no apparent negative correlation between the collapse of trade on the one hand, and the presence of international value chains in total trade, on the other hand. Moreover, this would seem to be a robust conclusion because it appears for different indicators, different samples and different trade flows. One should, however, remember that also these data present a partial relationship between two variables only. Further investigation is necessary in order to take other potentially relevant explanatory variables on board. Only then does a basis exist to reach a sensible empirical conclusion. Fortunately a number of more complete analyses are available and this is the topic of the next subsections (but also note that Chapter 7 will provide a multiple regression that meets these very reasonable requirements).

Single Country Studies

The study by Levchenko et al. (2009) was already discussed in the previous chapter (Section 3 in particular regarding trade credit). The study provides a detailed cross-section analysis for the US at the sector level of the factors that determine the extent of the reduction of bilateral US exports and imports between June 2008 and June 2009 and tests three different hypotheses for the trade collapse: compositional differences in demand (both by sector and final demand category), variations in the level of trade credit, and the occurrence of international value chains (vertical production linkages). Levchenko et al. (2009) investigate several indicators for vertical linkage: (i) the intensity with which goods are used as intermediate inputs, (ii) the number of sectors that use some good as an intermediate input and (iii) the concentration of downstream use measured with a Herfindahl index. These factors are generally found to be highly significant in equations that relate import decline to vertical linkages and a subset of product and industry characteristics (including the size of the sector, the labour intensity of production and the possibilities for substitution). For exports, however, hardly any significant relationship could be established. Moreover there is 'no evidence that measures of production sharing based on trade within the multinational firms are significantly correlated with a drop in international trade' (Levchenko et al., 2009, p. 17). Measures of upstream use (such as the intermediate use intensity and the number of intermediates used) are significant and negative, as expected. The estimated coefficients, however, show considerable variation and are no longer significant once the set of explanatory variables includes the structure of demand and the availability of credit (Levchenko et al, 2009, Table 10, p. 35).

Figure 4.6 illustrates some of the findings by Levchenko et al. derived from their decomposition of the aggregate reduction in US exports and imports and is based on their preferred parameter estimates. Interestingly, the econometrically estimated impact of both upstream and downstream linkages is not only more significant but its share is also larger for imports than for exports (note that this is also relevant in view of Chapter 7 where we will investigate import developments of 45 countries). For both flows we see that upstream linkages (where the estimated coefficients are not significant) are associated with three to four times stronger declines in trade than downstream linkages (which are actually significant in all specifications). The upshot is that the econometric evidence is weak where linkages could be empirically and economically relevant while it is strong where the effects do not seem to matter a lot.

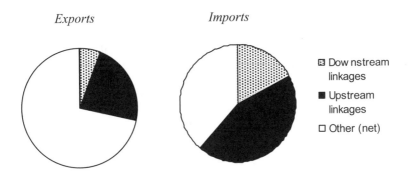

Source: Levchenko et al. (2009), Table 11, p. 36

Figure 4.6   *Contribution of downstream and upstream linkages to aggregate reduction in US trade*

Robertson (2009) provides some sort of a mirror analysis for Mexico, a country for which the US is a major trading partner. He argues that the importance of the export-processing 'maquiladora' trade with the US is the major cause of the collapse of Mexican trade. While Mexican trade hardly responded during the 1991 recession in the US, it contracted significantly in 2001 and even stronger in 2008. Robertson relates this to 'change in production structure that followed the North American Free Trade Agreement (NAFTA) in 1994'. It is beyond doubt that further international specialization is a consequence of economic integration (and this may to a large extent explain why Mexican trade flows collapsed), but it does not prove that the collapse was so strong due to the particular form of the international division of labour between the US and Mexico.

All in all, the single country approach provides no convincing evidence that being part of an international supply chain increases a country's vulnerability since exports are not hit more strongly if there are forward and backward linkages. Indications do, however, exist that international value chains are associated with stronger reductions in US imports.

Calibrated Simulation Models

Bénassy-Quéré et al. (2009) use the computable general equilibrium model MIRAGE to analyse the contribution of global supply chains to the world trade collapse. A computable general equilibrium model can deal with changes in behaviour of economic subjects (demand, supply, substitution), markets (relative prices, imperfect competition) and capital (investment, skills, etc.). MIRAGE covers many aspects that are potentially relevant for our discussion, including a calibrated pause in globalization, the development of the oil prices and properly modelled inter-industrial relationships (both inter-industry trade and own imports). But as always some crucial elements are missing as the authors themselves note. These missing factors include trade finance, inventory adjustments, a trend break (rather than a pause) in the globalization process and shifts in expectations. Since the model fails to replicate the strong fall in world trade, Bénassy-Quéré et al. (2009) conclude that the over-shooting in trade adjustment must be related to these omitted variables. (Incidentally, other omitted variables that are not on their list could of course also have been the drivers behind the depth of the trade collapse.) Although this conclusion is not logically sound in its wording (the model might simply be wrong, for example), the research does provide corroborative evidence that the fragmentation of value chains alone does not offer the explanation for the strength of the trade collapse.[11]

4. CONCLUSION

Perhaps the reader is a bit disappointed with the results of this chapter which all seem to be rather negative. The empirical evidence for the hypothesis that the strength and speed of the world trade collapse was caused by the fragmentation of production after all is not very conclusive. This is true for all the important building blocks of the hypothesis and at all levels of the analysis of value chains and value chain activities as we saw in the previous sections. To some this may seem to be an unsatisfactory outcome of the research. On a positive note, however, this is the way knowledge is generated in the social sciences. Hypotheses are formulated and then tested. Often the theories are refuted and this stimulates the formulation of new hypotheses which in their turn are tested, etc. Also note that the verdict that the empirical evidence is inconclusive differs qualitatively and importantly from the negative finding on trade finance and trade credit that we derived in the previous chapter.

Indeed, the potential empirical irrelevance of value chains is quite a remarkable and exciting finding because of the profession's early and outspoken conviction that supply chains were a (if not *the*) driver of the extraordinary trade developments in late 2008 and early 2009. The irrelevance of supply chains in explanations of the trade collapse thus is highly relevant. Policy advice early in the trade downturn must have been influenced by this narrative. At least two points are worth emphasizing because of their clear policy implications. Firstly, international value chains may actually have supported international business-to-business markets during the trade collapse. This may have been due to the fact that such value chains breed trust amongst firms because of the long-run character of their trade relationships or it may be a consequence of the negative correlation between individual preferences for protectionism and intra-industry trade which has smaller effects on the income distribution (see, on the latter, for example Melgar et al. 2009). Secondly, the return to the *status quo ante* may not be as quick as has been predicted, also because reactivation of value chains that have been broken or frozen will be a gradual process (Escaith 2009, p. 9). This suggests as a minimum that additional efforts are in order to increase trust in the trading system and that the period in which government policies will have to support and guide market processes could be longer than expected at the start of 2010.

In the final chapter we will investigate more closely some of the policy advice that was provided during the early phase of the downturn in the trade cycle and we will do so in relationship to the policy implications if this advice has been wrong-footed. Before doing so, however, we will have to consider two other potentially relevant explanations: protectionism and trade uncertainty and test competing potentially relevant hypotheses in a multi-factor setting.

NOTES

[1] See, for example, McLaren (2000) who theoretically derives an inverse relationship where openness drives the thickness of the market for intermediate inputs which facilitates 'leaner, less integrated firms'.

[2] Interestingly, Cheung and Guichard (2009, p. 15) state that they found coefficients that have the incorrect sign ('and are thus not reported' – *sic*) suggesting that an increase in vertical supply integration actually reduced the elasticity of trade with respect to GDP. The fascinating point here obviously is that the 'wrong' sign may be the right one depending on the view that one has on the role of global value chains and on their impact on trade.

[3] This is another subject for which statistical observations are very difficult to obtain.

[4] Escaith (2009, p. 4) uses the metaphor of an additional layer of transmitters that operates at the micro level. The new element is that information (shocks) does not only flow from client to producer, but also the other way round.

[5] It is still not clear what has been driving the de-stocking in these global value chains. Peels et al. suggest that this may have been a result of the credit crunch requiring divestment and a stronger focus on cash, but van Leeuwe (2009) and van Leeuwe and Bruinshoofd (2009) do not find a significant impact of stocks on international trade.

[6] An early contribution that analyses some of the complexities of this issue is McLaren (2000).

[7] This argument differs from the statistically oriented argument in Bénassy-Quéré et al. (2009) and O'Rourke (2009) that the elasticity of world trade to output may be stable even when the value of the world-trade-to-GDP ratio is higher due to fragmentation.

[8] No data on vertical specialization in trade were available for Iceland and Chile.

[9] The Grubel-Lloyd index measures intra-industry trade at the level of individual products as $1 - (|X-M|)/(X+M)$.

[10] Note that this implies that the primary data sources are also quite different, in particular because CPB estimates price components in order to deflate nominal trade data (van Welzenis and Suyker 2005) whereas the methodology in this book relies on locally estimated import price deflators.

[11] Interestingly, the same can be said of the other large-scale modelling exercise on this topic by Bems, Johnson and Yi who reach conclusions in favour of the value chain hypothesis. According to their Figure 9 (Bems et al. 2010, p. 40), however, only 4.1 percentage points of the trade decline can be attributed to trade in intermediate goods.

5. Protectionism is Just Around the Corner!

Before taking off, a sobering note is in order: economists are alarmists when they discuss the threat of protectionism. It often takes an outsider to see this. The political scientist Goldstein (1986, p. 163) noted the over-prediction of protectionism by the economic profession especially in the context of generally speaking liberal trade policies and wondered why 'such an inordinate amount of intellectual energy and time [has] been spent on worrying about the "slippery slope" [of protectionism]' Her verdict is clear: 'The continual reappearance of these predictions points to a series of flaws in the contemporary analyses of trade policy.' Of course the low level of protectionism could also be a self-denying prophecy reflecting that the warnings of economists are taken seriously.

Anyhow let us see why the economic profession is always so much concerned about protectionism and consider how economists analyse the occurrence of anti free trade policies. One of the key lessons from the 1930s on which all economists pretty much agree is that protectionism was one of the ugly aspects of economic policies in the interbellum. The narrative that is in the back of each economist's mind is that tariffs and non-tariff barriers helped to turn the Wall Street crisis from a financial crisis into the Great Depression. It is essentially this lesson that beggar-thy-neighbourism was disastrous in the 1930s which is behind all pledges against protectionism in the wake of recent G20 meetings. At the same time, however, one has to note that concrete actions to strengthen the open multilateral trading system apparently were too difficult. After all the world leaders were unable to reach agreement on the completion of the Doha trade round. From the start of the trade collapse there has been growing fear amongst international trade analysts that protectionism would sneak in and grow in the wake of the crisis. The sector-specific bailout packages targeted at crisis-hit companies, such as support for individual automobile firms, could trigger countervailing measures. More in general politicians could be expected to be under pressure to protect jobs at home. 'Buy local' pleas and laws are often seen. Are these only local incidents? Or is this the start of a new wave of protectionism?

Protectionism can be broadly defined as the set of economic policies that aim at restraining trade and investment flows coming into the economy. The focus of the analysis should be broad as both in the 1930s and during the trade collapse that started in 2008 many instruments were used. Commenting on the recent stance in trade policy Evenett (2009, p.7) notes:

> Focusing on a few policy instruments (...) therefore is likely to provide an inaccurate impression of the prevalence of, and probably the harm done by contemporary protectionism. A cumulative picture ought to be developed.

The methods of protectionism are wide and diverse as policy makers have been very inventive in finding new ways to hinder imports and incoming FDI: tariffs (border taxes), quota (limitations on the amount of goods to be imported), quality and technical requirements, certification and other forms of red tape, maxima set to foreign ownership, minimal local content requirements, commercial policies, subsidies and so on. Box 5.1 provides an overview of protectionist measures that are considered harmful to other countries.

Box 5.1   The ten most observed state measures to discriminate against foreign commercial interest since the first G20 meeting

The Global Trade Alert (http://www.globaltradealert.org) is an independent monitor of state measures that is constructed by an international group of trade policy analysts. The alert was launched in June 2009. It provides a good overview with much detail about the kind and numbers of protectionist measures, the countries that are involved in implementing the measures and the victims as well as a sector breakdown. At the first anniversary of the trade collapse in October 2009 the following top ten (by use) of measures could be noted:

1   Bailout/state aid measures
2   Tariff measures
3   Trade defence measures (such as an anti-dumping measures)
4   Public procurement/buy national policies
5   Non-tariff barriers (not otherwise specified)
6   Sanitary and phytosanitary measures
7   Export subsidies
8   Migration measures
9   Export tax or export restrictions
10 Import bans

Source: Evenett (2009), Table 2, p. 18

Typically, protectionist instruments are used in a discriminatory way against foreign companies thus distorting the level playing field. Often local regulations also act as a non-tariff barrier to trade and invest even though they are applied to all companies be they local or foreign. The reason is that the local company has to meet only one set of criteria, whereas a foreign company's product will have to meet the requirements of at least two markets (the home and foreign market). Such forms of protectionism are hidden and difficult to detect, but they do matter a lot. It should be noted that Box 5.1 only lists the kind of observable instruments and thus neglects the more circumspect impact of hidden protectionism which may be reflected in subtle shifts in preferences for locally produced goods and services – without a formal policy measure that can be observed and counted. Political speeches may, for example, contain explicit and implicit elements of calls to 'buy domestic'. Anyhow, the fact that the top three of the measures is dominated by state interventions that give the implementing institutes a lot of discretion (read: 'room for arbitrary decisions') led to concerns of 'murky protectionism' (Evenett 2009, p. 7).[1]

Let us now turn to the determinants and empirics of protectionism in order to glean some potential directions in which the conditions for global trade might develop. This chapter is structured as follows. Section 1 discusses the determinants of protectionism, both in a more or less purely economic sense and in psychological terms of the factors that impact on individual preferences. Section 2 discusses the development of protectionism during trade collapses and in particular takes stock of the analysis of the 1930s. Section 3 numerically describes some of the main trends and patterns in recent protectionism. By way of conclusion and using the findings in the earlier sections as a basis, Section 4 sketches three scenarios for the course of protectionism.

1. DRIVERS OF PROTECTIONISM

What then are the determinants of protectionism? We can answer this question at three levels. The first level is the level of the political economy of trade and commercial policies. This level provides much of the theories that economists use to analyse trade and commercial policies. It should be noted that the problem of increasing protectionism in the wake of a global recession with collapsing international trade and investment flows is not simply the mirror image of the problems that occur in the context of increasing growth and trade flows that have usually been analysed in economics. Still the main findings of the analysis of protectionism under the latter conditions are worth repeating. The second level starts from the recognition that trade restrictions are highly correlated with political support among national residents. It is therefore interesting to see how these preferences come about and to try to measure the key individual characteristics that make a person protectionist in attitude. Of particular relevance may be to see how macroeconomic and structural conditions have an impact on the individual's preference for or against protectionism. The third level takes game theoretic aspects into account,that is the strategic interaction between nation states and its impact on the formulation of bilateral and multilateral trade policies.

Political Economy of Trade and Commercial Policies

Typically the key assumption behind the international political economy analysis of protectionism and trade liberalization is that policymaking is rational. Policy decisions reflect the impact of trade on different groups that vote or lobby in order to get those policies imposed that maximize their welfare (sometimes only one ideal type of voter is studied: the median voter that can swing the decision either way). Trade liberalization would increase imports and thus competition from abroad and this would reduce rents (both of employers and employees) in sectors that were previously sheltered. These sectors, their firms, their workers and their organizations could thus be expected to be against trade liberalization and pro protectionist measures. Likewise, export sectors that stand to gain from market access due to liberalization of international trade could be expected to oppose protectionist measures and to be pro free trade. This manner of analysis also provides the insight that sector-specificity may explain the trade preferences of different actors in the economy (the capital owners, unskilled workers, skilled workers, and so on) depending on the question of how the relative scarcity of the respective actors' factor of production is influenced. How trade impacts on relative scarcity crucially depends on the assumptions that are being made about the mobility of the factors of production. In the standard Heckscher-Ohlin model that is the hobby horse for international economics and that assumes perfect mobility of the factors of production inside countries and perfect immobility between countries, unskilled workers in countries that are abundant in unskilled labour would be expected to benefit from trade liberalization and thus be against protectionism (and capital owners and high-skilled workers would be expected to favour protectionist trade policies in such countries). But if mobility inside countries is less than perfect because it is costly to move or to adjust (human) capital so that it could be used in other industries, then the opposite outcome would result.

It is not obvious if this kind of modelling offers the right kind of answer to the analysis of protectionism in an environment of declines in production and increases in unemployment because this environment would seem to correspond with an economy that is not at the production frontier and/or is characterized by substantial friction unemployment during periods of substantial change in the extent of international specialization. Despite these remarks one of the key ideas of the modelling approach would still be valid, namely that support for free trade would be a consequence of the gains from trade. The point is of course that the world trade collapse substantially reduces these gains from trade. Indeed factors of production that can no longer be employed in export-oriented industries will by necessity have to move to import-competing industries thus further and more structurally undercutting opposition against protectionist measures.

A complicating issue is that large countries would relatively stand to benefit from a return of trade barriers, including higher tariffs. The theory of the optimal tariff (also known as the terms-of-trade argument) states that large countries can use their market power in world markets to shift the terms of trade in their favour. Small economies would thus have to bear a relatively larger part of the reduction in global welfare caused by an increase of protectionist measures.[2] Comparable profit-shifting occurs in 'strategic trade policy' models that mainly deal with the industrial sectors that have been hit the most during the trade collapse. Large countries could be tempted to resort to protectionist measures. Moreover, the balance of small and large countries shifted due to European integration and the advent of China.

At yet another level, policy choices and the resultant constraints on the policy space may be relevant for the decision to use the only alternative available, that is protectionism. Eichengreen and Irwin (2009) econometrically analysed the drivers behind the tariff escalation in the 1930s, finding that protectionism increased especially in those countries that had themselves substantially restrained their other policy options regarding the exchange rate and fiscal and monetary policy instruments, for example by strict adherence to the Gold Standard. This finding could also become relevant in modern times (although in a different disguise), for example, for the countries that have joined the European Monetary Union. The ECB has a reputation as a fierce defender of price stability. As a consequence of the financial crisis global inflation was subdued in 2008 and 2009, so monetary policy in Europe could be relaxed. A weakening of the euro exchange rate and/or an increase in commodity process (in particular of oil) could, however, force the ECB to increase interest rates again. Moreover, EMU's Stability and Growth Pact constrains the fiscal room of manoeuvre for its member countries, making this a relevant issue: both factors restrict the policy mix.

Preference for Protectionism

The availability of international survey data on economic policy preferences has enabled another, empirically oriented research strategy that deals with the determinants of individual preferences. Examples of this manner of highly innovative research include amongst others O'Rourke and Sinnott (2001), Mayda and Rodrik (2005) and Melgar et al. (2009). Typically such research tries to explain normalized scores obtained for questions such as 'Respondent's country should limit the import of foreign products in order to protect its national economy' (this is the question that is investigated by all of these three studies) or 'Do you think it is better if (1) goods made in other countries can be imported and sold here if people want to buy them; or that (2) there should be stricter limits on selling foreign goods here to protect the jobs of people in this country' (this question is investigated by Mayda and Rodrik 2005). Survey data are now available for a sufficiently large number of developed and emerging countries although it should be noted that data for developing countries are still relatively scarce.

O'Rourke and Sinnott (2001) related protectionist attitudes to nationalism and patriotism (so ideology rather than the material interests). Using a data set for 24 countries in the 1995 International Social Survey Programme they find a significant and quantitatively important impact for these attitudes. They also uncover other still not well understood correlates that also have been confirmed in later studies such as a positive correlate between gender, age and protectionist preferences (females and elderly tend to be significantly more protectionist than young males). Still O'Rourke and Sinnott find that skills and education are also very important for understanding why some people favour protectionism and others support free trade. This effect is more significant and important in countries with a relative high level of per capita income. (Note that the latter effects are in line with the Heckscher-Ohlin models that we discussed earlier.) These results are broadly in line with Mayda and Rodrik (2005) who analyse two data sets (23 countries in the 1995 International Social Survey Programme and 47 countries in the 1995–1997 World Values Survey). The use of the latter source is important as it uses a different question and covers more developing countries. One important finding is that individual preferences can to a significant extent be explained by individual human capital (education levels and pro free trade preferences are positively correlated) and the kind of industry in which people work (import-competing employment correlates positively with a preference for protectionism). The factor-endowments (skills) and specific-factors (sector of occupation) models survive a joint test (although some of the variables are only significant at the 90 per cent confidence level).

In addition to the individual preferences, Melgar et al. (2009) consider the impact of macroeconomic conditions (such as average growth, inflation, import penetration and the export-to-GDP ratio). The non-economic drivers of the individual trade policy preferences identified in this analysis of the International Social Survey Programme for the year 2003 confirm earlier findings based on other data sets. The formation of preferences is influenced by social status and relative income (middle and upper class people are more likely to be pro free trade), values (religion and protectionist preference are positively correlated) and attachments ('think-local'-ists and nationalists tend to be anti free trade). One particular relevant driver may in theory be the feedback from protectionist measures to individual preferences but this is not supported by the data. Finally, education provides a strong antidote against protectionism. The macroeconomic drivers are interesting because these could be expected to be especially relevant during a period of trade collapse when growth turns negative. The macroeconomic variables are, however, insignificant with the exception of inflation and the sector structure (farmers and their employees are more protectionist than those working in industries and occupations in the services sector are least protectionist). Individual unemployment – another consequence of financial crises – does not have a significant impact on protectionist preferences, but working in the more flexible segments of the labour market (such as part-time work) does significantly impact on a person's trade policy preferences.

The conclusion is that personal characteristics, beliefs and attachments are important determinants of individual protectionist preferences. Such determinants are unlikely to shift during an economic crisis and this can provide some sort of stability. The economic theories that relate an individual's support for free trade to the individual's gains from trade are however also relevant. Reallocation of labour between sectors and a reduction of foreign markets may thus shift preferences from free trade towards protectionism.

Retaliation

One lesson of the 1930s is that countries often retaliate against perceived protectionist behaviour by imposing tariffs and other non-tariff barriers to trade themselves in response to foreign legislation that breaches free trade principles. The most well known example is the Smoot-Hawley Act that the US imposed in June 1930 and that set higher tariffs for agricultural and industrial products. According to WTO (2007, p. 42)

> The passage of the Smoot-Hawley Act and the retaliatory response it engendered are considered a classic example of the disastrous repercussions of unilateral protectionist actions on international trade relations and the volume of trade flows. The protectionist measures introduced unilaterally by the strongest economy at that time, which was also the largest international creditor with a large trade surplus, did not produce the intended [domestic] results [for the US] (.., I)mportantly Smoot-Hawley shattered the limited trust remaining in the trading system and wrought havoc on global trade flows.

The fact that Smoot-Hawley was an important trade event in the interwar period is beyond dispute, but it is equally important that it was followed by similar British legislation in 1931 and 1932.[3] All these events sparked a wave of protectionism around the world. The escalation of tariffs during this period was, however, general and not specifically targeted against the US or the UK thus reflecting that policy makers were acting against all foreign trade which they saw as being detrimental to their own economic development.

How do countries get stuck in trade wars? Consider Table 5.1 which lists the pay-offs of two large countries (country A; country B). The symmetry in the pay-offs is not relevant and only for convenience. These countries have to choose between two policies: free trade and protectionism. If the countries both follow a free trade policy their pay-off is 110; if they both opt for protectionism their pay-off is lower at 100. The countries are large because they can influence their own pay-off if they impose protectionist measures: if country A opts for protectionism while country B opts for free trade the pay-off of country A increases to 120 while country B's pay-off reduces to 90. (And it could also be the other way round of course.) Countries have to decide on the extent of international specialization before they know the policy choice of the other country and therefore it is sad but wise to assume that the other country will be protectionist.[4] Given that assumption it is again sad but wise to opt for protectionism. Thus both country A and country B opt for the protectionist policy although they could do better if they cooperated and followed an internationally coordinated free trade policy.

Table 5.1 Game theoretic perspective on trade wars

| | | Country A | |
		Free trade	Protectionism
Country B	Free trade	(110; 110)	(90; 120)
	Protectionism	(120; 90)	(100; 100)

It is often argued that the threat of countermeasures has also helped countries to stay on an anti-protectionist track. It is indeed true that a tit-for-tat strategy ('if you impose protectionist measures in this period I will do the same in the next period') provides an important incentive against the imposition of trade barriers. This can be illustrated by playing the game described in Table 5.1 repeatedly and possibly indefinitely (it then becomes a so-called super-game). Assume that the countries are free traders. The first year first-mover gain of protectionism would amount to 10 (=120−110), but now it has to be balanced against the losses endured during all later years of −10 (=100−110). In this hypothetical case protectionism has a higher net present value only when discount rates are high so that future losses are discounted. Unfortunately, short-sightedness is not uncommon, especially amongst politicians that have to win the next election, and during crises when policy makers may simply discard future consequences in order to solve emergencies. Moreover, in case of failure the retaliation threat has to be executed. One only needs one irresponsible large actor to shift the world economy towards the protectionist equilibrium.

2. EMPIRICS OF PROTECTIONISM AND TRADE COLLAPSE

It may seem astonishing, but the actual impact of protectionism and its drivers in the interbellum are still a subject of recent debates amongst economists. One reason is that more sophisticated methods of analysis allow researchers to take a fresh look at the facts, while the increase in computing power and the availability of newly developed data sets make it possible to test alternative hypotheses. Two examples are Madsen (2001) and Estevadeordal et al. (2003).[5] Madsen provides an econometric test of the significance of tariffs and non-tariff barriers in the interbellum using a time-series approach for a panel consisting of the 17 major trading nations. Moreover, Madsen attempts to find out by how much protectionist measures and other potentially relevant explanatory variables (in particular the decline in GDP) contributed to the decline of the world trade volume (Table 5.2). A critique of the study could be that non-tariff barriers are estimated using time dummies, rather than using direct observations on quota or the rationing of foreign exchange. This means that the estimate for the non-tariff barriers may be contaminated and relate to other not-included variables.

Table 5.2   Causes for the decline of world trade in the interbellum and their contribution to that decline (1929–1932)

Cause	Percentage reduction of world trade
Declining income	14
Discretionary increases in tariffs	8
Endogenous deflation induced increases in tariffs	5
Imposition of non-tariff barriers	6

Source: Madsen (2001)

Estevadeordal et al. (2003) reach opposite results using a different methodology and a different sample of countries. They analyse trade developments between 1870 and 1938 in a gravity model for 28 countries and the years 1913, 1928 and 1938 and use the estimated model to decompose the contribution by separate factors using observations for the explanatory variables for 56 countries in five benchmark years (1870, 1900, 1913, 1929 and 1938). Note that the use of benchmark years implies that their analysis does not pertain to the actual downturn in trade (so from peak to trough) but rather considers a peak to 'partial recovery' movement (compare Figure 2.1 and Table 2.4 and the discussion in Section 4 of Chapter 2).[6] Estevadeordal et al. indentify an increase in transportation costs and the demise of the Gold Standard as the main driving forces of the decline in world trade volumes and conclude that

> Tariffs may explain some of the fall in trade after 1914. But they are not the whole story, and other frictions helped reverse the trend growth of trade in the interwar period (Estevadeordal et al. 2003, p. 391).

Recent empirical research may disagree on the actual impact of protectionism in the interbellum, but there is agreement that the trade collapse was not sparked by an increase in protectionism, which Madsen (2001), Estevadeordal et al. (2003) and Eichengreen and Irwin (2009) date around 1931–1932. Rather protectionism according to these studies could thus be seen to have been caused by the combination of declines in income and the collapse of world trade. The 2008–2009 trade collapse was not much different in this respect. It took place at a moment in time when trade policies were generally speaking liberal. There is some evidence that protectionist pressures were building up during 2009 as we will see in Section 3 below, but there is no evidence that protectionism was a problem early on in the trade decline.[7] All in all, the following quote from Bénassy-Quéré et al. (2009, p. 10) would seem to neatly summarize the profession's verdict on the role of protectionism before, during and following the onset of the trade collapse:

> Emerging protectionism is unlikely to have contributed to the collapse of world trade observed at the end of 2008, but it may have a sizeable impact in 2009 and 2010, when the social consequences of the crisis in the real economy (...) will be felt and subsequent demands for protection can be expected. So far, it must be said that the monitoring process performed by the WTO seems to have kept such risks under tight control.

Although protectionism occurred only on a limited scale of local incidents the risks of a wave of beggar-thy-neighbour policies is lurking. Thus, for example, Cernat (2009) concludes that the risk of the emergence of more trade restrictive/distortive measures is not behind us – even though he acknowledges both that considerable constraint was exercised in the deployment of the trade policy instruments and that the impact of border measures on EU trade interests was quite limited (he estimates that up to roughly 4–5 per cent of EU exports could be affected).

3. RECENT PATTERNS OF PROTECTIONISM

This section summarizes and analyses some of the data that have been reported in the Global Trade Alert data base, which is the leading data set for protectionism during the 2008–2009 trade collapse (see Evenett 2009 for a discussion). The Global Trade Alert is a very useful initiative that provides a monitor of state measures related to trade and investment or that influence international exchange indirectly via their impact on the level playing field. Of course the initiative aims at creating greater awareness for such measures and the hope is that the transparency about protectionist measures will help to contain trade barriers. At the same time transparency makes the actions visible that could ignite a wave of protectionism.

Potential Data Problems

Although the data base of the Global Trade Alert provides the best and most comprehensive overview of state measures since mid 2009 two problems should be noted. The data collection is partly driven by reports and this may of course introduce some selectivity. It may pay firms and/or governments to complain in order to put pressure on other governments. Obviously the Global Trade Alert team checks all complaints and if claims are not justified then such complaints will be classified as non-discriminatory. Yet it is unavoidable that some bias is introduced since measures that do not distort trade and/or actually involve liberalization and greater transparency will in all likelihood be underreported. Another problem with the Global Trade Alert monitor should, however, also be clearly recognized. Its dataset only contains observations during the trade collapse and provides no benchmark for earlier periods. Therefore it is difficult to see trends and often it appears that some conclusions (although possibly true) do not follow logically from the data set.[8] The time series available in 2010 was still too short to make the necessary corrections for seasonal variation in the observed planning and implementation of protectionist measures. This may be relevant because during the holiday season, for example, no bureaucrats are available to do the red tape of implementing the measures in the pipeline.[9] Fluctuations in the number of implemented measures should be corrected for seasonal influences.

A related problem is of course that due to the short period of its existence relatively little experience exists in analysing the data beyond the level of descriptive statistics and that cross-checks to other types of data such as events data related to international conflict and cooperation have yet to be made. Also due to the delay in reported trade statistics it is impossible to link these economic data to the data in the Global Trade Alert. The latter are collected over the internet and via other media so that they provide almost a real-time description of protectionism. The mismatch in timing between economic data and the Global Trade Alert data on protectionism will change in the future when levels and instruments can be tested on their impact on trade and investment flows.[10]

Some Trends in Modern Protectionism

Still it is possible to glean some intriguing trends in state measures as for example illustrated in Figure 5.1 which analyses the number of state measures actually implemented in the eight months before and the state measures considered at the end of February 2010.

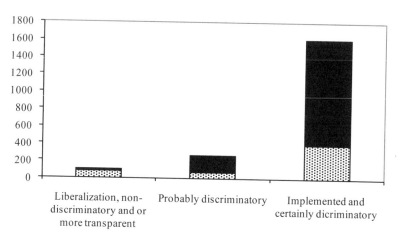

Note: The categories follow the classification in the Global Trade Alert (from left to right 'green', 'amber' and 'red')

Source: Global Trade Alert database accessed on 24 February 2010

Figure 5.1 Total state measures reported by the Global Trade Alert initiative

Figure 5.1 allows a few interesting observations. First of all one notes that the state measures are predominantly of a discriminatory nature. Some 95 per cent of all the implemented and considered state measures that had been identified by the end of February 2010 are in this category of harmful discrimination.

Secondly, however, some of the observed measures are neutral or actually support trade because they involve liberalization or an increase in transparency of policy instruments. This rather optimistic picture is, however, only possibly relevant for 2009 as illustrated by the measures that were actually implemented. For 2010 and beyond pessimism is the more relevant attitude. Indeed, whereas 85 per cent of the previously implemented measures are (definitely or most probably) discriminatory against the commercial interests of foreign firms, 98 per cent of the measures in the pipeline fitted into this category. This was not only due to the stark increase in the number of discriminatory measures, but the reduction in the share of non-discriminatory measures is also caused by the drying up of the measures aimed at liberalization and greater transparency.

Thirdly, an enormous amount of protectionism was obviously hanging above the market by the end of February 2010. If implemented the number of protectionist measures would increase three-fold.

Table 5.3 Top ten of countries imposing discriminatory state measures

No.	Implementing jurisdiction	Number of state measures	Number of tariff lines affected[*]
1	Russian Federation	56	486
2	United States of America	54	124
3	Argentina	50	92
4	India	48	212
5	Germany	39	22
6	United Kingdom	32	133
7	China	29	334
8	Italy	28	25
9	Spain	27	47
10	Hungary	26	18

Note: * Measures that are certainly discriminating against foreign commercial interests and that have been implemented by the specified jurisdiction

Source: Global Trade Alert database accessed on 24 February 2010

On the Brink of Deglobalization

Culprits and Victims

Table 5.3 lists the ten countries that imposed the largest amount of discriminatory trade measures in the nine months preceding February 2009 and the number of the tariff lines that were affected by those implemented measures that were judged 'certainly discriminatory'. Typically the large economies are almost all in the game of protectionism. It should be noted with respect to Table 5.3 (and 5.4 as well) that the number of measures does not translate one to one into the impact of protectionism (that is the amount of harm done), because this depends on the type of measure and the actual amount of trade involved.

Table 5.4 provides the mirror image by means of a list of the ten countries that were hit most by discriminatory trade measures in the nine months preceding February 2009 (the table also summarizes the number of jurisdictions imposing these measures). The top ten involves the world's major trading nations as could be expected if one assumes that successful trade activity breeds protectionist countermeasures.[11] Also noteworthy is that measures against Asian economies appear to have been taken by relatively many countries. This would not seem to be driven by retaliation as these economies with the exception of China do not appear in Table 5.3.

Table 5.4 Top ten of countries targeted by state measures

No. Country		Number of jurisdictions imposing
1 China	322	62
2 Germany	194	36
3 United States of America	188	52
4 France	172	37
5 Italy	161	32
6 United Kingdom	159	35
7 Japan	158	50
8 Belgium	155	33
9 Netherlands	148	35
10 Republic of Korea	138	47

Source: Global Trade Alert database accessed on 24 February 2010

It is too early to tell from these snapshots how protectionism will develop in the aftermath of the world trade collapse. Several possible states of the world can be discerned depending on whether protectionism continues to be contained or whether the disease spreads. This is the topic of the final section that sketches three scenarios for trade policies beyond 2010.

4. THREE SCENARIOS FOR TRADE BEYOND 2010

Scenarios are useful tools if the future direction of the economy is very uncertain. In the context of the world trade collapse this analytical instrument is particularly relevant given the unique character of the event and because the theoretical and empirical perspectives differ so much. The three scenarios to be sketched in this section combine coherent perspectives that each use different assumptions about underlying economic processes and the uncertain development of the parameters, but they do not provide predictions. Often knowledge depends on recent post-Second World War experiences and it is not clear whether these regularities will be applicable to the situation of stagnant growth and trade – especially if the duration for this context is extended over longer periods than previously experienced. Rather than providing predictions, the scenarios explore possible futures that can realistically be expected given the available knowledge. With this caveat in mind we can now take a look at the three scenarios 'Lessons learned', 'Bashing China' and 'Tsunami of protectionism'.

Scenario 1 Lessons Learned

The first scenario is quite optimistic. It assumes that world leaders understand the importance of free international trade for the health of all economies, including their own economy.

Building blocks
The first assumption underlying this scenario is thus that policy makers and politicians take the lessons of the 1930s to heart and that they also understand that the collapse of their export markets in 2009 has not been caused by protectionist measures. A second element that this scenario reflects is the observation that economists and political scientists have a bad track record of over-predicting protectionism. Therefore this scenario is cautious, assuming little protectionism. A third, empirical, building block consists of the assessment that protectionism in 2009 has been local and incidental rather than structural. Finally, the scenario reflects the econometric finding that individual preferences for protectionism have not significantly been influenced by average economic growth and unemployment.

Opportunities and threats
The scenario does not guarantee a return to the *status quo ante*; it merely assumes that protectionism will not aggravate the situation. The global economy could thus also in this scenario be characterized by stagnant international exchange, possibly due to a reorientation of firms and

consumers towards local activities. The fact that protectionism does not poison international political and economic relations is a helpful factor of course as this enables international policy coordination and further cooperation.

Scenario 2 Bashing China

The second scenario is based on a continuation of the shifts in the geography of international trade that have led to China's status as the world largest exporter as of December 2009. Clearly this is a development that has already been in the books for quite some time, but its occurrence was shifted forward in time due to the world trade collapse. The scenario suggests that China's success generates political and economic dynamics that greatly increase the number of protectionist measures against this country.

Building blocks

The first building block is that China has become a very relevant player in the world economy and power politics and power economics are thus to be considered – probably 'Realist' defence issues need to be taken on board as well. An important intellectual building block of this scenario is provided by international profit-shifting theories such as the theory of the optimal tariff and strategic trade theories. This would seem to be a relevant element because China is a large economy and this may induce other large economies such as the US (or the EU) to counterbalance perceived Chinese market power especially if competitive success of the Chinese economy is seen as the result of unfair competition from state-owned companies or as a consequence of Chinese trade and exchange rate policies. An editorial in *The Economist* (6 February 2010, p. 9) describes several aspects of this scenario:

> It is in the economic field that perhaps the biggest danger lies. Already the Obama administration has shown itself too ready to resort to trade sanctions against China. If China now does the same using a political pretext, while the cheapness of its currency keeps its trade surplus large, it is easy to imagine a clamour in [US] Congress for retaliation met by a further Chinese nationalist backlash.

An important empirical building block for this scenario is the observation that China in 2009 appeared to be the number one victim in terms of the number of measures imposed against it by other countries.

Opportunities and threats

In the coming decades the group of old trading nations of Europe and North America that shaped the rules of that system loses its majority share in world trade and production. Thus the historical, cultural and institutional background of emerging economies could change how the world defines and settles international economic disputes. The clearest danger in this scenario is therefore that it alienates one of the largest emerging economies from the multilateral trade system and thereby in the longer run puts free trade at serious risk.

Scenario 3 Tsunami of Protectionism

The third scenario assumes that the potential of protectionism that is hanging above the market is unleashed. This may be due to a further deterioration of economic conditions but also some specific event could act as a trigger of retaliation around the world.

Building blocks

The first, empirical, building block is the potential of a three-fold increase in protectionist measures. All drivers of protectionism become relevant in this scenario, including the lack of (or drying up of) other options in the policy mix as well as the recognition of a game-theoretic context in which one event sparks a wave of retaliation. The spread of protectionism in this scenario would go beyond actual trade restrictions and also influence individual preferences in an anti free trade direction, thus exercising additional pressure on politicians to take a firm stance against foreign commercial interests.

> In sum, foreign products are seen as a threat to national production, more than an opportunity for consumers and strategic aspects of trade policies seem to matter for the public opinion. Consequently, there are a wide range of circumstances such as recessions that may increase protectionism pressures; pressures which could quickly spread from one country to another (Melgar et al. 2009, p. 20).

Opportunities and threats

The scenario is grim and implies that openness declines in line with world trade. Second-order effects will feed back and result in subdued growth and possibly yield W-shaped recessions of production and trade. The most important consequence, however, is that international co-operation breaks down and that it will be difficult to restore trust among nations. This spread of distrust may not be limited to global institutions but could also involve forms of regional cooperation.

Possible Futures

As said before, these scenarios sketch possible futures. One way to judge the likelihood of the scenarios is to watch out for signals that could be related to a scenario. A clear signal, for example, for the first scenario would consist of a successful completion of the Doha Round of multilateral trade negotiations. A relative strong increase in the number of protectionist measures specifically targeted against China would provide an observable indication for the second scenario. A continuing upward trend in state measures that discriminate against foreign commercial interests and are not targeted against specific countries would provide an empirical indication that the third scenario is relevant, especially if some form of escalation occurred. Of course none of the scenarios claims to represent the true future – the point is that scenarios provide some sort of benchmark situation and that their probabilities (or the weights attached to the scenarios) are subjective and dependent on available information. As new information becomes available we will have to reconsider our opinion.

NOTES

[1] The term 'murky protectionism' was coined by Baldwin and Evenett (2009).

[2] Potentially policy relevant applications of the theory of the optimal tariff are also related to scarce essential raw materials such as the 'rare earths' that are very important in the production of microelectronic equipment or to energy. Tariffs could be used to counterbalance monopoly power. A tax on greenhouse gas emissions (which are ultimately related to the consumption of gas and oil) could thus shift monopoly rents from the OPEC countries to the OECD countries.

[3] See, for example, Kindleberger 1973, pp. 128–35.

[4] This point is discussed in more detail in the next chapter.

[5] Note that we discussed these studies already to some extent in Chapter 1.

[6] Another complicating factor for their counterfactual is that the share of world trade covered by the sample reduces from 95 per cent in 1910 to 85 per cent by 1939, due to the creation and disappearance of countries (as well as changes in their territories) which is a particularly relevant factor given that this period covers the First World War and the interbellum.

[7] Note that Jacks et al. (2009) find that broadly defined trade costs increased prior to 2009.

[8] An example is Evenett's (2010, p. 2) observation that discrimination against foreign products in 2009 was much higher than originally reported. From this he concludes 'Any suggestion that 2009 was a benign, low protectionism era should be dismissed'. This conclusion cannot logically be drawn unless data for earlier years are available.

[9] During a presentation of the Global Trade Alert at VNO/NCW (November 12, 2009) in The Hague the chairman Martin van den Berg joked that this provides the argument *par excellence* for much longer holidays for trade policy makers.

[10] An early analysis that uses these data is Jacks et al. (2009).

[11] This would happen in the case of endogenous trade uncertainty which is discussed in Chapter 6.

6. An Alternative Hypothesis: The Forgotten Role of Trade Uncertainty

The trade collapse arrived out of the blue. Professional traders and economists were completely surprised by a decline in trading opportunities of this magnitude. The decline was global in nature as no country escaped from the fact that its customers and/or its suppliers were in serious trouble. Accordingly thrust in international trade decreased and risk appetites dampened thus further strengthening the atmosphere of economic insecurity. As pointed out earlier it is exactly this fact that constitutes one of the key potential drivers of the world trade collapse that has have been overlooked: the actual implementation of trading decisions became much more uncertain. We have encountered this deep-seated uncertainty and many of its manifestations in previous chapters. The payment system, country risks, protectionism in the pipeline – all these factors make the arrival of goods and/or the receipt of international payments insecure.

Thus trade uncertainty in the context of a global crisis is fundamental and it occurs on all levels of analysis. Will trading partners still exist when the goods arrive? Will the goods arrive? Will trading partners be able to pay? Admittedly, uncertainty is always a fact of life in international economic relations. Volatility of exchange rates, of (relative) prices and of trade flows in general influence the decisions of private firms and consumers and, consequently, determine (the possibilities for) foreign trade (see, for example, Ruffin 1974; Pomery 1984 and Kofman et al. 1990). Moreover, as international payments need to be made it is not only the individual firm's capacity to pay that matters, but also its bank and even its home country. National policies are important because unsustainable policies put the exchange rate at risk and induce capital controls and import restrictions. (The case of Greece in the spring of 2010 illustrates that even the national policies of one country may endanger the exchange rate of other countries.) Moreover, countries could be expected to increase protectionism to engage in competitive devaluations during and in the aftermath of financial crises. While most of the literature considers uncertainty as an exogenous phenomenon (at least as unrelated to the levels of consumption, production, trade and so on), Bhagwati and Srinivasan (1976) have argued that the possibility of quantitative trade restrictions (import quotas, voluntary export

111

restrictions, boycotts and embargoes) may also be affected by the volume of one's exports so that large traders may encounter larger risks of trade disruption and therefore international trade is more vulnerable than domestic trade in times of crisis.

All these international factors, so to say, add to the normal business risk. Indeed, if anything, the crisis must have increased the subjectively perceived risk that international trade will be disrupted. Therefore trade uncertainty must be key to understanding the speed and significance of the strong trade collapse both in the 1930s and in 2008–2009.

Why Was Uncertainty Overlooked?

Someone might want to object that it is highly unlikely that trade uncertainty is a relevant empirical issue given the lack of attention for this topic in the policy analyses of the international organizations. After all: how could a factor that is so fundamental be disregarded by the whole profession of international trade economists? This is a relevant objection, but still the fact that this factor has been neglected remains on the table and in the end its statistical significance and economic relevance are empirical issues that we will address in Chapter 7.

One possible explanation for the neglect of this factor is that no data are available that can be used to actually measure the extent of trade uncertainty (although a lack of data for trade finance and value chains, as we have seen before, did not stop theorizing and policy advice on *those* issues). So perhaps another explanation is that the dominant approach in modern trade analysis has not (yet) been much concerned with this issue.

Top empirical research in international economics is investigating micro data (so observations at the level of individual firm) and the theoretical paradigm centres round the heterogeneity of firms. It is not the case that no micro data sets have been analysed in contexts characterized by financial stress. Examples of micro data studies that deal with financial shocks are Choi and Kim (2003) and Bricogne et al. (2009). The point is rather that uncertainty *per se* had not been explicitly considered in a fundamental way and on a broader basis. The heterogeneity approach provides a very successful research agenda: the growing availability of national panel micro data sets that deal with the internationalization of firms has increased understanding of, and interest in, the impact of international trade and investment on performance of firms. Firms that export, import, invest or have a head office in other countries are more productive, larger, do more research and development, have a higher survival rate and pay better wages than firms that are only connected to local markets. International trade analysts are increasingly appreciating that the differences and complexities of economic agents under the heading 'heterogeneity' make a break with the representative firm paradigm unavoidable. A useful review of the emerging (empirical) literature is Wagner (2007).[1] Of course as is the case with all shifts in economic paradigms new knowledge builds abruptly but does not cover all (sub)fields at once. So at the outbreak of the world trade collapse the mini-revolution of firm heterogeneity in international economics had not yet been able to deal already with the issue of trade uncertainty in a more fundamental manner. For example, Segura-Cayuela and Vilarrubia (2008, pp. 8 and 10) point out that 'this ingredient appears to have been largely overlooked by the literature'.

This is a fair judgement for the heterogeneity school but not so for the more traditional neoclassical theory that deals with exogenous and endogenous uncertain trade (see van Marrewijk and van Bergeijk 1990 and 1993 and van Bergeijk 2009a, especially Chapter 3).

Section 1 discusses the theory of trade uncertainty in the context of the well-known neo-classical trade model. (Non-technical readers may want to skip this section and the next one although the theoretical analysis is always verbal and graphical and does not require any knowledge of mathematics; they can proceed to Section 3.) Section 2 discusses some extensions of this model focussing on the question of how the decision-making structure of an economy (that is whether it is an autocratic, centralized and/or planning economy or a decentralized, democratic and/or market economy) relates to the extent of (de)specialization in the context of potential trade disruption. One important theoretical finding is the existence of an information (or co-ordination) externality in decentralized market economies that induces too strong an international specialization pattern in such economies. Section 3 discusses some stylized facts and alternative theories that may yield similar relationships between specialization and political structures. Section 4 draws some theoretical conclusions and investigates the normative implications for trade policy.

1. THE THEORY OF TRADE UNCERTAINTY

How do perceptions of increased trade uncertainty influence actually observed trade volumes? It is helpful to analyse this issue by first taking a look at the mirror image of trade disruption – that is the well established case of the movement from autarky to free trade. This approach helps to clarify concepts and the method of analysis. Then we will turn our attention to trade uncertainty *per se* – and we will discover that the mirror images are not completely symmetrical: the economy-wide extent of de-specialization in international specialization overshoots even if firms and consumers do not show such behaviour at the individual level. Trade uncertainty thus is shown to be a phenomenon worthy of analysis on its own merits.

From Autarky to Free Trade

So let us see what the traditional neoclassical model that is based on a representative firm and a representative consumer tells us about the impact of changes in the level of international trade.

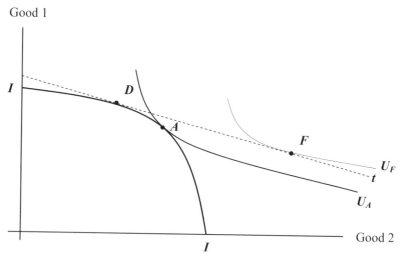

Figure 6.1 The neoclassical model: from autarky to free trade

We start by considering Figure 6.1 that illustrates this model for a small open economy that trade two goods. The production structure is represented by a transformation curve *II* that represents all efficient combinations of good 1 and good 2 that the economy can produce. The preferences of the consumers are represented by indifference curves that have been identified with the utility levels U_F (of free trade) and U_A (of autarky), respectively. The economy trades at the international price ratio *t*, that shows the relative price of good 1 and good 2 in the international market. The economy is small and thus cannot influence this price ratio by its supply and demand.

Three points are of special interest: the autarky point *A* (where the economy consumes what it domestically produces), the free trade consumption point *F* and the concomitant production point *D* (the economy specializes in the production of good 1 which it exports and exchanges against good 2). Note that utility in *F* exceeds utility in *A* which in its turn exceeds utility in *D*.

The comparative static analysis of free trade is part and parcel of 'International Economics 101', but how does the autarkic economy reach free trade? What happens when we move from *A* to *D* in production and from *A* to *F* in consumption? Figure 6.2 illustrates the time path of utility. A jump in utility occurs and then as the economy specializes (this takes some time) the free trade utility level is approached. These images of the benefits of free trade are in the back of every economist's mind, but how does trade uncertainty work out in this scheme?

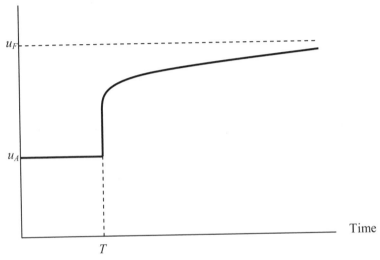

Figure 6.2   Time path of utility as the economy moves from autarky to free trade

The least complicated and most transparent way to introduce trade uncertainty in the neoclassical trade model is to assume that two states of the world exist: a free trade environment where all trade is possible and a no-trade environment where all trade collapses (van Marrewijk and van Bergeijk, 1990). This abstraction of course does not imply that actually no trade will occur – it should be interpreted as describing the views of the economic subjects (firms, consumers, government) on the future state of the economy. This view or perception can be expressed in terms of a weighted average of these two extreme states of the world. Next it is also important to realize that an economy or its agents decide on the pattern of domestic specialization before the state of the world is known (that is whether a no-trade or a free trade situation occurs). Once the decision about the optimal pattern of specialization has been taken either by a social planner or decentralized through the market mechanism, the allocation of the factors of production cannot be changed overnight because of the costs of reallocation or, alternatively, the time needed to make adjustments.

The Case of Trade Disruption

These theoretical building blocks are shown in Figure 6.3 that illustrates that international specialization in conformity with comparative advantage does not always yield a utility outcome that improves on the benchmark welfare level that would be reached in the case of autarky. So countries that fully specialize may end up at a lower level of utility then when they had a priori decided not to trade at all. Whether this paradoxical outcome results or not depends on the particular trade regime that occurs after the economy has decided on its specialization pattern. In the free trade situation the economy consumes in point F and achieves the maximum level of utility attainable U_F. But if the no-trade situation emerges while the economy is fully specialized, production is at D because the factors of production have been used in specific combinations and reallocation will take time and imply high costs. By necessity consumption drops to D, the production combination that is actually being produced. Since this production combination is the result of decisions that assumed that international trade would be possible, the resulting consumption combination logically cannot be optimal if trade is impossible.

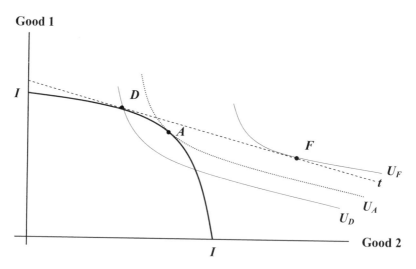

Figure 6.3 Trade disruption in the neo-classical model

The extent of international specialization is thus suboptimal if the originally expected volume of international trade does not materialize and this situation will yield a lower utility level (actually even less than in autarky). Consequently, the next step in the model is that the economy will start to de-specialize in the no trade environment. The optimal point in the no-trade situation is autarky *A* but the economy will not reach that point instantaneously, because the reallocation of the factors of production will take some time.

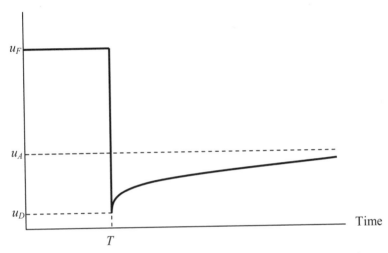

Figure 6.4   Time path of utility as the economy moves from free trade to autarky

From this story we can deduce the time path of utility which is directly related to the consumption possibilities in the economy and shows the abrupt drop from point *F* to point *D* and then the more gradual movement towards point *A*. The time path of utility (Figure 6.4) is thus not the mirror image of the movement from autarky to free trade (Figure 6.2) although free trade and autarky are the beginning and end points of the time paths.

The Model and Some of the Stylized Facts of Trade Collapse

Simple as the model may be, it offers a helpful tool if we want to understand what kind of observations regarding the trade collapse are worth further investigation and which are not (or alternatively, from which observations we can actually draw meaningful conclusions). Take, for example, the weight that observers (as we earlier saw in Chapters 1 and 4) have put on the fact that trade fluctuated much more strongly than production. This is not quite as extraordinarily as many seem to have been thinking – at least not from the comparative statics perspective on which the present chapter is based. It is directly obvious from Figure 6.3 that the maximum fluctuation in production (from *D* to *A*) along the production possibilities frontier *II* is much smaller than the maximum fluctuation in trade (from point *F* to *D*), basically because the economy's production fluctuates between the production point of free trade and the production point in autarky while trade fluctuates from the maximum free trade volume to nil. Likewise, the observation that the trade multiplier effect during the trade collapse is smaller if GDP is measured at current prices is quite in line with this chapter's model.[2] The movement along the production possibilities frontier at domestic prices is smaller because the the economy de-specializes (it produces less of good 1 and more of good 2 in Figure 6.3) and the price ratio changes from the tangent in point *D* (international prices) to that in point *A* (see also Section 2 below). Consequently, income at national prices decreases more quickly.[3]

We can also deduce a few points from the time path of utility in Figure 6.4. Firstly, it is interesting to note that the neoclassical analysis of a shock increase in trade uncertainty shows that 'green shoots' are not necessarily a sign of improvement. After all utility in this model starts to increase again after time *T*, but the illness of this economy is not cured at all and the *status quo ante* is never restored. In other words, green shoots indicate the start of an adjustment process, but they do not necessarily indicate that the economy is improving and actually is on a long-term track towards a better situation than before the trade shock occurred.

Secondly, and more importantly, consumers and producers will consider the expected utility of their consumption and production decisions and will *a priori* prefer a pattern of international specialization between autarky and free and undisturbed trade. Trade uncertainty thus yields less specialization in accordance with (and perhaps even against) comparative advantage and hence trade uncertainty induces a reduction of international trading opportunities and global welfare (van Marrewijk and van Bergeijk 1993). That is to say that they would prefer a point between *D* and *A* in Figure 6.3 depending on the (implicit and/or subjective) probabilities that they attach to the respective trade regimes. If they expect the no-trade regime to occur in the next period they will specialize in point *A* and if they expect the free trade regime they will specialize in point *D*. Setting these limiting cases aside they will prefer a position in between and would like to be more located towards *A* if they think that trade is more uncertain.

The expectation mechanism has a powerful impact on trade indeed. Even if trade continues to be free and undisturbed *ex post*, we will measure a reduction of trade once perceived uncertainty increases *ex ante* because the specialization in production will shift towards point *A*. It should, moreover, be pointed out that specialization may actually go against comparative advantage in the case of endogenous trade uncertainty (that is when the probability that trade is limited depends on the volume of trade). Endogenous trade uncertainty is by no means a merely theoretical possibility, as illustrated by Table 5.2 that shows that all major trading nations are in the top ten of countries that most often fell victim to protectionist measures during the trade collapse.

All in all these neoclassical insights would seem to be crucial both in understanding what is happening in the world economy and to inform and design economic policy responses to deglobalization.

Caveat: From Theory to Observation

A clear problem with the theory of trade uncertainty is of course that trade uncertainty is not readily observed. We do not have surveys where people are asked how likely they believe that trade disruption in the next period will be. We can only observe the direct reaction of economic subjects, that is the actual development of trade flows. Perhaps we can also observe changes that occur in the pattern of specialization, but it has to be noted that it will take quite some time before the detailed statistical information will become available.

It would thus be useful if we could relate the reaction to economy-specific characteristics. Since we want to explain the strength and speed of the movement from the previous free trade equilibrium towards a new equilibrium (in which trade is much more uncertain), it seems logical to pay attention to the coordination and decision-making mechanisms in the economy. Such institutional features of the economy can be observed and would both form a basis for policy advice and could guide econometric design. Typically one can observe these institutional features along different dimensions (Table 6.1): decision-making, political structure and the prevalent coordination mechanism of the economy.

Table 6.1 Institutional features

Decision-making	Centralized	Decentralized
Political structure	Autocratic	Democratic
Economic coordination	Planning	Market

Of course Table 6.1 gives the extremes of the archetypes along these three dimensions that we will study in the next section. This is not because I deny that reality is much more complex showing all kinds of nuances (and often also many apparent inconsistencies). The purpose of the focus on the extremes is to make the analysis as transparent and clear as possible. Later in Chapter 7 when we put the theoretical insights to the test we will use scales and combinations of these institutional dimensions. But for now, let us see how changes in specialization can be influenced by the extent to which the decision-making process is centralized or decentralized or the extent to which structures are autocratic or democratic.

2. TRADE UNCERTAINTY, INTERNATIONAL SPECIALIZATION AND DECISION-MAKING

Having discussed the theoretical setting in the traditional neo-classical model, it is now time to complicate the analysis a bit further in order to introduce country-specific characteristics into the analysis. The reason is that we want to understand why, as illustrated in Chapter 2, country experiences during trade collapses differ to a large extent. Which type of economy adjusts sub-optimally? Will a decentralized market economy produce at the optimal point of production? This is a relevant question since producers and consumers face given prices if markets are characterized by perfect competition. If we ignore the limiting cases where either free trade or autarky is certain, then a private decentralized economy will probably not produce at the point that would be optimal given the concomitant probabilities.

The point of departure is the logic that consumers and producers will consider the expected utility of their consumption and production decisions and will *a priori* prefer a pattern of international specialization between autarky and free and undisturbed international trade, but their decisions can only be optimal if they can take the impact of their decisions on each other into account or if they can rely on a third party (for example, the government) that coordinates their responses taking their preferences into account. If this is not the case then an externality exists that renders the outcome of their decisions suboptimal from a national welfare point of view.

Consider Figure 6.5 that illustrates the decisions that firms and consumers face. Both producers and consumers incorporate the possibility of a no-trade and a free trade regime into their decisions. If the free trade regime prevails, consumers maximize utility in point F where the price ratio equals the international terms of trade p_W. In the no-trade regime, however, the consumption combination D results, which given the indifference curves, will yield the domestic price ratio p_d. Rational risk-averse utility-maximizing households will prefer a price ratio between p_W and p_d; that is a production combination between point D and point G (where the transformation curve is tangent to the no-trade domestic price ratio). Producers on markets that are characterized by free competition face the choice between point G which would maximize their profits if the domestic no-trade price ratio equals p_d and point *D* which maximizes their profits in the free trade regime. So like consumers in this decentralized economy, expected profit-maximizing firms will choose a production combination between *D* and *G*.

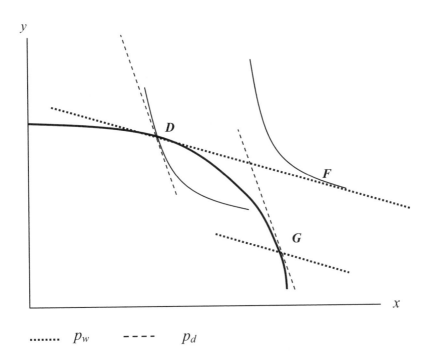

Figure 6.5   Prices and quantities that play a role in the consumer and producer decisions

There is, however, no reason why consumers and producers even for given and identical subjective probabilities would hold identical preferences about the optimal point of production. Under certainty the standard neoclassical model formally optimizes production and consumption in two steps. That is to say, production is first chosen so as to maximize national income for given technologies and given world prices. Next, consumption is determined given domestic production, world prices and consumer preferences. Once uncertainty is introduced, the optimality of this procedure may break down, as production decisions need no longer be consistent with consumption decisions.

The implication is that decentralized economies will trade too much in relation to the existing trade uncertainty – which is sub-optimal – and will thus have a larger drop in welfare than the centralized decision making economy if the no-trade regime occurs.

3. EMPIRICS OF THE TRADE–DEMOCRACY NEXUS

The theoretical findings in the previous two sections imply that autocratic, centrally-planned economies, due to their centralized decision-making processes, will respond more adequately to an increase in trade uncertainty. Because they do not have to rely on the implicit coordination between firms and consumers to reach the optimum level of specialization they move faster and consequently reduce and reorient their external trade at shorter notice. Consequently, the international specialization of these countries would be relatively limited.

An example is the external trade by the member countries of the former COMECON, the East Block's trading association during the superpower conflict of the Cold War. Already well before the fall of the Iron Curtain observers noted the much lesser extent of international specialization *vis-à-vis* market economies. Marer (1985, pp. 98–9) summarized the consensus of experts on the trade participation ratios of centrally planned economies as the trade-to-national-production ratio being 'certainly not higher and almost probably lower, than those of market economies of approximately the same size and development level'. Once the countries in the former East Block started to integrate in the world economic system, many studies proved this consensus right and also the data confirmed the verdict: trade volumes 'exploded' at double digit growth rates, both with the OECD (East–West trade) and amongst the formerly planned economies (East–East trade).[4]

This relationship between trade orientation and the political system has also to some extent been observed during periods of world trade collapse. In the previous chapter we encountered a recent example when we observed that Russia is heading the top ten of countries that imposed the largest number of trade restrictions and it also achieved a number one position in the number of tariff lines involved (see Table 5.3). In the 1930s this relationship also appears to have existed. Discussing the choice of instrumental variables in their study on the drivers behind the tariff escalation in the 1930s, Eichengreen and Irwin (2009, p. 26 footnote 39) note:

> One might plausibly think that countries with authoritarian political regimes would be more likely to resort to exchange controls; restrictions on political freedom tended to go together in this as in other periods

Actually, they report that this political variable works nearly as well in the econometric exercises as their preferred economic instrument variable. So for both world trade collapses we have some corroborative evidence for the influence of decision-making, political structure and the prevalent co-ordination mechanism of the economy. Some evidence also exists on the relationship between democracy and trade policy at the level of individual preferences. Investigating individual trade policy preferences Mayda and Rodrik (2005) have found a correlation between pride in a country's democracy and pro-trade attitudes.[5] They take this 'to indicate that trade is less threatening to individuals who have confidence in their country's political institutions' (Mayda and Rodrik 2005, p. 1410).

Democracy and Trade Policy

It should be noted that these empirical regularities and stylized facts do not *prove* that the theory of trade uncertainty is right. In particular other theories may be able to explain the relationship between the extent of international specialization and the institutional set-up of countries. Recent literature has studied two issues: (i) the relationship between democratization and trade policy where the driving mechanisms are the marginal voter and changes in the number of people allowed to participate in the vote and (ii) the impact of autocratic rule where the driving mechanisms are the dictator's ability to extract rents by use of policy distortions and a lack of control on red tape and other trade barriers due to a lack of political accountability in autocratically ruled economies.

Democratization and trade policy

O'Rourke (2006) provides a discussion of the literature on the relationship between trade liberalization and democratization. He develops a median voter framework that he links to the Heckscher-Ohlin model. Increases in the share of the population that is allowed to vote would give more weight to labour and thus the gains from trade that can be reaped by labour should to a larger extent determine if trade policy is liberal or protectionist. Democracies that are labour scarce would be more likely to be protectionist and labour-abundant economies would be more likely to be pro free trade. He tests the democracy–free trade link for a sample of 35 countries in the period 1870–1914, using several versions of the model and providing many checks on robustness. O'Rourke finds no evidence for a simple relationship between democratization and trade liberalization and only uncovers a significant impact in a model that includes land–labour and capital–labour ratios.[6] According to this model democratization and trade liberalization are more strongly correlated in rich, capital-abundant countries. For the more recent period 1970–1990, Milner and Kubota (2005), however, find in a sample of 179 developing countries (that is to say, for poor, capital-scarce countries) that shifts in trade policy in the direction of free trade are also significantly associated with shift towards (more) democratic institutions.

The theory of trade uncertainty differs from this theory of democratization and trade liberalization in two important respects. Firstly, the model that is used in this chapter is a bit more general in nature as it also applies outside the context of Heckscher-Ohlin. Secondly, the theory of trade uncertainty does not investigate the impact of changes in the 'level' of democracy. It relates the extent of the adjustment in international specialization to the manner of decision-making and the coordination mechanism in the economy.

Autocratic rulers
Aidt and Gassebner (2007) follow a different line of thought as they see the possibility of a dictatorial ruler to extract rents by imposing trade distortions as the driving mechanism (and additionally they argue that control and monitoring of trade policies are less well developed in autocracies). Their model provides a versatile testing ground in a gravity model that studies 130 countries over the years 1962–2000. One of the key empirical findings is that the level of trade in an autocracy is about a fifth lower than the level in democracies after controlling for country characteristics and implemented trade policy regimes. In a practical sense this theory is less naïve than the theory of trade uncertainty since Aidt and Gassebner take into account that bureaucrats and politicians in autocratically ruled countries need not be benign social planners that work for the good for all. In a theoretical sense, however, their model is restrictive because it requires a distortion between the private benefit of the ruler and success of the exporting sector and also because it introduces a specific assumption regarding the possibility to monitor and manage trade policy bureaucrats. The theory of trade uncertainty does not require such additional assumptions regarding the quality of institutions: its merit basically is that it points out the existence of a market failure (the uncertainty externality) that was not recognized but will occur in general although in differing degrees.

4. CONCLUSIONS AND IMPLICATIONS FOR POLICY

So what have we learned and how does this relate to the world trade collapse? My point in this chapter has been that the economic context is characterized by an upward shift in perceived risks of international trade, that is an increase in trade uncertainty. Introducing uncertainty with respect to the trade volume in a traditional neoclassical trade model for a small open economy yields less specialization in accordance with (and perhaps even against) comparative advantage. The practical implication of this theoretical finding is a reduction in the international trading opportunities. Although the following was not formally shown in this chapter at a global level (as the model relates to a nation) it is worth pointing out that the reduction in international trade opportunities implies both lower national and global welfare. It may be a comfort to the reader that these results have been shown to be independent of the number of goods that are considered in the analysis, the extent to which economic decision making has been centralized or decentralized, or the question of whether this uncertainty is exogenous (that is 'systemic') or endogenous ('trade volume-related'). The results are thus more general than suggested by the simple model that was used to present the basic theoretical concepts.[7]

Regarding (trade) policy making we were also able to derive a number of conclusions. A first conclusion is that in the decentralized private market economy government intervention *could* improve on welfare by coordinating economic decisions whenever uncertainty exists with respect to the future trading climate. Trade uncertainty is a market distortion and public intervention is thus legitimate provided that the benefits of coordination (that is removing this distortion) exceed the costs of public actions and instruments. It is important to note that a general argument based on (endogenous) trade uncertainty and the deployment of the incentives such as quantity controls, border taxes or subsidies can in practice hardly be distinguished empirically from trade interventionism which is guided by the 'new trade theory'.[8] This is especially the case when endogenous trade uncertainty is a consequence of commercial activities by foreign competitors on the world market and addressed in a bilateral framework. The upshot is: firstly, that measures to reduce the externalities of trade uncertainty may often be perceived as protectionist measures; secondly, that proposed measures should be analysed empirically in order to establish that they actually work; and thirdly, that a cost-benefit analysis is appropriate to establish that the costs of solving the market failure do not exceed the benefits of reduced trade uncertainty.

The second conclusion from this chapter is that first-best government action therefore should be aimed at reducing uncertainty *per se*, possibly through strict adherence to conflict settlement procedures and a completion of the Doha round that would at least signal commitment to free trade and multi-lateral conflict resolution. Indeed, such policies tackle directly one of the sources of the problem from which the uncertainty externality arises in the first place.

NOTES

[1]   One issue in this literature that may become relevant in the context of the trade collapse resolves around the question of where the well established macroeconomic welfare of more openness derives from if firms do not become more productive while they internationalize their commercial activities (this is a key finding of micro data studies into the behaviour of heterogeneous firms). The point is that the micro–macro paradox of international economics can be reconciled when we consider the effects of industry restructuring; that is that more productive firms drive out less productive firms. This adjustment process to globalization and its impact on Total Factor Productivity plays an important role in recent theoretical models (Melitz 2003, and for a more elaborate analysis that in addition shows that the effects are stronger in sectors with comparative advantages: Bernard et al. 2008). Accordingly trade turbulence during a trade collapse can have a significant impact on productivity

[2]   The observation is, for example, made by Bénassy-Quéré et al. (2009).

[3]   The difference between GDP at domestic prices and GDP at international prices is one intuitive explanation why economies that face substantial trade uncertainty may specialize against comparative advantage (see van Marrewijk and van Bergeijk 1993).

[4]   Afman and Maurel (2010) discuss the development of East–West and East–East trade in the 1990s.

[5]   This study was discussed in more detail in Chapter 5, Section 1.

[6]   The data set for this model is somewhat limited due to data deficiencies but it is not completely clear how this influences O'Rourke's results.

[7]   See van Bergeijk (2009a, Chapter 3) on all these issues.

[8]   See van Bergeijk and Kabel (1993) on the strategic trade literature and Dixit (1990) for a critical evaluation of proposed government interventions when private firms fail to deal with trade uncertainty (for example due to non-observability of individual actions, outcomes and characteristics). Indeed according to Dixit (1990, p. 18) trade taxes and subsidies are justified 'only if a transaction were to affect [the probability of trade disruption] by its inherent cross-border nature'.

7. Let Us Test the Theories

An important finding in Chapter 2 of this book has been that the world trade collapse experience is not homogeneous across countries. Although this would seem to be fairly obvious, it still is perhaps the most important stylized fact that we uncovered: individual country experiences differ a lot, both in terms of duration and depth of the import crunch. So while all countries almost simultaneously experienced a decline in international trade, specific country characteristics appear to have determined to what extent the trade volumes of individual countries collapsed. This is by no means a unique aspect of the recent world trade collapse. Chapter 2 provided detailed evidence for this heterogeneity during the world trade collapse in the 1930s (Figure 2.7 and Table 2.4), during the individual financial crises in the 1980–2007 period (Figure 2.5 and Table 2.3) and also during the 2008–2009 trade collapse (Figure 2.9 and the summary Table 2.5). Chapter 2 noted that asymmetric falls in trade did not seem to be correlated with exposure to the crisis in any simple and straightforward manner. One implication of the observation that all countries shared the common experience of trade collapse while the extent to which trade was reduced differed considerably at the same time, however, is obvious. Under the veil of the common experience there must be significant heterogeneity in the underlying shocks, transmission mechanisms and/or (structural) country characteristics.

One aim of this book is to uncover the impact and relevance of such factors. Now that we have discussed the long list of potential explanations (that is the potential drivers) for the trade collapse in Chapters 3–6 it is therefore tempting to make an empirical attempt at sorting out this variation in observed depth and duration and analyse why these country experiences diverged so substantially. Therefore this chapter will endeavour to test the key elements of the dominant narrative that developed in early 2009 amongst trade economists.

Section 1 introduces and recapitulates the long list of potential explanations for the trade collapse and evaluates whether the potential explanation could make sense in order to arrive at a set of theories that can be put to the test. This section translates the theories that make it to this short list into empirically testable propositions and discusses the indicators that will be used in the econometric evaluation. (At the end of the chapter a data appendix is provided that discusses the sources and methods that have been used in the construction of the dependent and explanatory variables.) Section 2 introduces a simple cross-country regression as the basic methodology of this chapter and discusses the *a priori* expectations regarding the impact of the explanatory variables. Section 3 presents the empirical results of a set of relatively simple regression analyses that try to determine the factors behind both the depth and the duration of the import collapse of 45 countries in the period 2007–2009. Section 4 draws conclusions setting the stage for Chapter 8 where we will discuss policy issues.

1. LET US ASSUME THE WTO IS WRONG: 6 + 1 HYPOTHESES FOR THE WORLD TRADE COLLAPSE

It is useful to choose one of the early 2009 narratives for the world trade collapse, as an organizing principle to provide the structure for the discussion in this chapter. I will use one of the flagship publications of the World Trade Organisation, the *World Trade Report 2009* (WTO 2009b, pp. 2 and 18, note that the full text is reproduced in Box 1.1), which suggests six explanations for the strength of the trade collapse:

- the decrease of commodity prices,
- swings in the value of the US dollar,
- the concurrence of problems in all countries,
- the presence of global supply chains,
- shortage of trade finance, and
- an increase in protectionism.

Let us consider in more detail which of these six hypotheses deserve a place on the short list of potentially relevant factors that we will use in an empirical analysis of the percentage decrease of the volumes of imports during 2007–2009Q3 in a group of 45 countries (these countries are listed in Table 7A.1 in the appendix).

Values Versus Volumes

The first two explanations in the *World Trade Report 2009* basically are irrelevant from my perspective. They relate to the monetary value of trade flows and these measurement issues do not have an impact on changes in import volumes which I plan to study in this chapter.[1] This is especially so because, as discussed in Chapter 1, values and volumes of world trade during the recent trade collapse appear to move more or less in tandem. Anyhow, since this chapter studies the changes in import volumes we will have to look for other reasons for the trade collapse.

Concurrence

The third explanation in the *World Trade Report 2009*, that is the fact that all countries were simultaneously hit by the crisis and reduced their imports, is of course relevant as this clearly limits export-oriented strategies aiming at growing out of the problems. Indeed, as argued earlier the global nature of the 2007 financial crisis, and especially the fact that most countries experience reduced demand at the same time, suggests that the duration of the trade collapse may become much longer than any post-Second World War episode. But concurrence is not a relevant aspect if one wants to investigate heterogeneity across countries. Concurrence may explain the average depth and duration of the world trade collapse, but not the individual country experiences.

Global Value Chains

The value chain argument has a strong intuitive appeal as we discussed in Chapter 4. This is mainly because so many well-known products are international composites. These complex products often have multinational supply lines and, moreover, many less important components are also produced all around the world. Two implications follow from the global value chain argument. Firstly, it entails an increased linkage of economies and thus the concurrence of collapse in many countries. This is relevant for the collapse of world trade in general but does not have a bearing on the observed heterogeneity of country experiences. Secondly, there is a measurement issue since components in the final product are counted every time they cross a frontier. Thus import and export data (which are turnover figures) may show stronger fluctuations than the underlying changes in final demand (which is a value added figure).

In Chapter 4 also some potentially counterbalancing impacts were identified such as the larger trust among repeat buyers and the use of non-bank-intermediated trade credit. Much trade is intra-company trade that takes place within multinational corporations that manage international value chains. These intra-company trade flows would seem to depend relatively speaking to a much smaller extent on trade credit or trust in general and this actually could mitigate the impact of the global financial crisis on international exchanges.

The upshot is that the direction of the impact of global value chains on trade during a global crisis is not *a priori* clear and essentially an empirical matter.

The global value chain argument, however, undoubtedly deserves a place on the shortlist because the extent to which these global value chains make up a share of trade flows differs a lot between countries. This heterogeneity is a consequence of, amongst others, the patterns of international specialization, comparative and competitive advantages and the dynamics and extent of intra-industry trade flows.

The value chain argument *à la* the *World Trade Report 2009* provides a clear and testable hypothesis, namely that trade in manufactured goods is especially vulnerable during trade collapses as these goods constitute the vast majority of the international composites.[2] I use the share of SITC6-8 in total imports as an indication of the intensity of a country's manufactured goods import.[3] I expect *a priori* that a larger share of manufactured goods will be associated with a stronger import reduction.

I also use the share of vertical specialization in trade (VSI) as an alternative measure which is of course more directly related to the issue at stake, but I can do so at an obvious cost only: the number of observations reduces to 34 countries when I use VSI as an explanatory variable.

Trade Finance

As discussed in Chapter 3 insufficient trade credit was 'a usual suspect' from the start of the world trade collapse. It is therefore no surprise to find trade finance on the WTO's longlist of potential explanations. At the time of writing, however, the evidence for this particular assumption is not convincing at all and especially so since causality is an issue. The conclusion of Chapter 3 was that trade finance by and large collapsed due to a lack of trade. It would therefore be inappropriate to include trade finance as an explanatory variable in an empirical investigation of import volumes.

Protectionism

The sixth explanation in the *World Trade Report 2009* actually is a warning. The Secretary-General of the WTO offered it as a potential explanation on a pre G20 press conference in March 2009 (WTO 2009a) but the WTO staff rephrased this hypothesis into a warning in the *World Trade Report 2009* in July 2009. The evidence that we discussed in Chapter 5 suggests that protectionism has occurred so far on a limited scale of local and individual incidents. If anything protectionism does not seem to have been a driver of the trade collapse.

This analysis is also put forward by the international organizations regarding other forms of international economic relationships. While acknowledging the risk of rising protectionism and some relevant policy tensions, UNCTAD (2009b, p. 15) for example concludes that 'no significant backlash against FDI has been observed so far'. All in all protectionism is not on our shortlist and I actually hope that this will remain the case.

Trade Uncertainty

The financial crisis must have increased the subjective probability that international trade will not occur. Trade uncertainty *per se* is difficult to observe so I will follow an indirect method to test the relevance of this hypothesis. As we saw in Chapter 6, one implication of the neoclassical model of trade uncertainty is that decentralized economies will tend to trade too much in relation to the existing trade uncertainty and to adjust too slowly. A shock in trade uncertainty will thus *ceteris paribus* lead to a stronger reduction of trade in a centralized economy. The extent to which decision-making in an economy is centralized or decentralized can be observed and if we hypothesize that trade uncertainty was global in nature (which is quite reasonable in view of our earlier discussions) then one would expect that the strength and speed of an import volume reaction will *ceteris paribus* be related to the decision-making characteristic of a country.

In order to take account of this characteristic of a country's decision-making structure I rely on the Polity database, an important data set constructed by political science (see Jaggers and Gurr, 1995) that provides scores for the extent to which a country's decision structure is autocratic or democratic and a combined measure that measures 'relative democracy'. I expect *a priori* that centralized decision making in the context of an increase in trade uncertainty will *ceteris paribus* yield lower levels of specialization and trade volumes and thus larger trade reductions. In other words I expect the depth of the import crunch to be smaller and its duration to be longer in countries that are characterized by decentralized (democratic) decision-making institutions.

2. EMPIRICAL DESIGN

Having discussed a number of potentially relevant explanations for the strength of the trade collapse, it is now time to take a closer look at the development of the import volumes of 45 countries in the period 2007–2009Q3 and to consider to what extent the suggested explanations are relevant. Given the observation that world trade appears to have bottomed out at the end of 2009, it would seem possible to analyse what factors correlate with the contraction of import volumes in this first phase of the trade cycle (that is from top or peak to bottom or trough). It is perhaps still impossible to say something meaningful about the recovery (or perhaps a further collapse) of trade flows, but the available data would seem to allow to answer in principle at least the question of why trade initially did collapse to this extent.

It should be noted from the start that this is a low pretence exercise that only aims to make a preliminary assessment of some empirical regularities in a dataset that will be updated and revised over the next quarters if not months. Perhaps someone would want to object that it is better to wait longer and then make a better analysis. However, if one wants to say something about the very recent developments, then there is no other option but to use whatever data are available, even if these data are imperfect and prone to revisions and updates. Moreover, I do not develop a formal model but will estimate a set of quasi-postulated reduced form equations that take account of some of the conflicting explanations that we discussed earlier (in particular the global value chain and trade uncertainty hypotheses) and also this lack of formal structure may attract criticism. For a preliminary assessment, however, the methodology suffices, as we will see.

Method and Explanatory Variables

The analysis takes the form of a cross-section analysis of the development of the volume of import that occurred between 2007Q1 and 2009Q3 in 45 countries. The development of imports is represented by two key variables: the depth of the import crunch (that is the percentage decrease of the volume of imports) and the duration (the period of decline measured in quarters). While depth is a measure of the amplitude of a cycle, duration measures the wavelength. It is well known from physics that both aspects of the cycle are related to the medium in which the 'wave' oscillates, in other words by the parameters that define the international context and the national country-specific characteristics. In this chapter we are interested in the national country-specific characteristics.

Based on our earlier discussion, the available data and their characteristics, I select four economic explanatory variables for the percentage reduction in import volume. Two of these variables are directly related to the hypotheses on our shortlist. The first variable is the share of manufactures before the start of the crisis or, alternatively, the share of vertical specialization in trade, and it is used to test the global value chain hypothesis. The second variable is the extent of (de)centralized decision making at the start of the crisis which is used to indirectly test the trade uncertainty hypothesis. These two variables are added to a *core* model.

In the core model for the depth of the import crunch two obvious economic variables play the main role: the reduction in the country's gross domestic product (GDP) that occurred between 2007Q1 and 2009Q3 and the country's inclination to import in the year before the crisis. GDP development and import inclination are not directly related to a particular hypothesis. Rather the inclusion of these variables provides a useful correction for a large number of economic country attributes that a priori would seem to be relevant for import volumes as explained below.

The core model for the duration of the import decline deploys one economic variable only (the import inclination ratio) and a measure related to the production speed of statistics, that is the publication delay. We now turn to a more detailed discussion of the three variables that appear in the core models.

GDP crunch

Inclusion of the GDP crunch (that is the percentage decrease of GDP between peak and trough as identified over its own cycle) is relatively straight-forward. Obviously, effective demand will be reduced when national income decreases and thus imports follow the development of GDP. As we discussed in Chapters 1 and 4 the consensus view sees income growth as one of the drivers of the second wave of the growth of world trade in the most recent phase of globalization, in particular due to the growing importance of international value chains. This consensus gave rise to the idea of a trade multiplier that magnifies fluctuations in income. The multiplier has been established at the time series level, but not in a cross-section setting as is being done in this chapter.

In principle I expect a positive correlation between changes in the import volume and changes in the real GDP level, but one can be even more strict because the mainstream argument is that imports will show stronger fluctuations than the underlying changes in final demand and this implies an expected coefficient (elasticity) in excess of one.

Import inclination

Import inclination is the comparative strength of a nation's intention to import. Some countries import relatively more than other countries, even after controlling for potential causes such as the geographic location (in particular the distances to other markets), the production level, the population size and being an island or a landlocked economy. One may even go deeper in one's efforts to understand why some trade flows are larger than expected and therefore also consider factors that are relevant at the bilateral level such as common languages, free trade agreements and exchange rate arrangements including monetary union. Even after controlling for all these factors we still have countries that import more than we would expect on the basis of these objective factors.

The extent to which this happens is measured by the trade inclination parameter. This variable is formally defined as the ratio of a country's actually observed bilateral import flows to the in-sample predictions for those flows (using an applied trade model), so that countries that trade more than expected are said to have a strong import inclination (for example, exceeding the value of one).[4] I expect *a priori* that countries with a strong import inclination will reduce their imports to a lesser extent than countries with a weak import inclination.[5]

Publication delay

A statistical issue is that not all countries in the sample had already published data for the third quarter of 2009. This is of course relevant since observations from the early phase of the trade collapse will generally speaking relate to smaller reductions of trade flows. Therefore a dummy variable was included to test whether publication delay (that is the number of quarters elapsed between the latest available number and 2009Q3) had an impact on the econometric results.

Estimated Equation and *a Priori* Expectations

All in all two quasi-reduced form equations will be estimated for the depth and duration of the observed real import crunch using Ordinary Least Squares:

$$\log{(\textit{import crunch})} = \alpha\, \textit{polity} + \beta \log{(\textit{value chain})} + \\ \gamma \log{(\textit{import inclination})} + \delta \log{(\textit{GDP crunch})} + \varepsilon \qquad (7.1)$$

$$\log{(\textit{duration})} = \theta\, \textit{polity} + \xi \log{(\textit{value chain})} + \\ \psi \log{(\textit{import inclination})} + \lambda\, \textit{delay} + \varepsilon \qquad (7.2)$$

With

import crunch	decrease in seasonally adjusted import volume in per cent, measured peak to trough and over the period 2007Q1–2009Q3,
duration	the period between peak and trough in quarters,
polity	the autocracy, democracy or relative democracy score that characterizes the extent of decentralized decision making related to the year 2007,
value chain	the share in per cent of SITC 6, 7 and 8 in total imports in the year 2007 (an alternative measure to be deployed is the share of vertical specialization in trade, VSI),

GDP crunch		the decrease in the seasonally adjusted volume of gross domestic product in per cent, measured peak to trough and over the period 2007Q1–2009Q3,
import inclination		the ratio of a country's actually observed bilateral import flows to the in-sample predictions, based on a gravity trade model, estimated for the year 2006,
delay		the number of quarters elapsed between the latest available number and 2009Q3, and
ε		the error term.

Note that all equations are formulated log-linearly. An advantage is that the estimated coefficients (with the exception of delay) can directly be interpreted as elasticities (so that an increase of, for example, GDP crunch by 1 per cent raises import crunch by δ per cent. A potential disadvantage is that the estimated relationship by assumption is multiplicative while an additive relationship *a priori* is equally probable (I will return to this point in the final section). The procedure involves estimation of different specifications of equations 7.1 and 7.2. The appendix to this chapter provides a detailed discussion of the variables, the data, the definitions and the countries that have been covered by the analysis. Table 7.1 provides a descriptive statistical overview of the data that will be analysed.

Table 7.1 Descriptive statistics for the dependent and explanatory variables

	N	Mean	Median	Max	Min	Std
Import crunch (%)	45	−24.0	−21.4	−10.0	−45.9	9.7
Duration (quarters)	45	4.2	4.0	9	1	1.7
Autocracy (score)	45	0.4	0	7	0	1.3
Democracy (score)	45	8.3	10	10	0	2.6
Relative democracy (score)	45	7.9	10	10	−7	3.7
Manufacturing share (%)	45	57.8	58.0	74.2	33.8	8.5
VSI (%)	34	26.5	26.0	54.9	10.9	11.7
Import inclination (ratio)	45	0.49	0.39	2.7	0.08	0.5
GDP crunch (%)	42	−8.2	−6.5	−2.1	−29	6.1
Delay (quarters)	45	0.38	0	2	0	0.5
Ongoing (dummy)	45	0.3	0	1	0	0.5

Notes: *N* is the number of countries for which data are available
Max is the maximum in the data set
Min is minimum and
Std is standard deviation

A priori expectations

Regarding the variables that appear in the core models the following hypotheses can be formulated. Firstly, I *a priori* expect that a reduction of GDP is associated with a reduction in import volume ($\delta > 0$), but it will also be important to test whether trade volume fluctuations exceed those of GDP (that is $\delta > 1$). Secondly, I assume that countries that are heavily inclined to import will *ceteris paribus* reduce their imports to a smaller extent, basically because many reasons to rely strongly on import will not change due to the crisis (a clear example is the geographical location or the need to import key raw materials such as oil). Therefore import crunch and import inclination will be negatively related (so I expect to find $\gamma < 0$). The impact of import inclination on duration is less straightforward. Open economies may try to keep trade channels open as long as possible while ultimately having to give in to the fact that economic activity is below trend (this suggests $\psi > 0$) but such economies may also be more responsive to positive news ('green shoots') and that suggests that the trough could be hit earlier (so $\psi < 0$). Clearly this is an empirical question. Thirdly, one expects that the longer the publication delay (that is the more the data relate to a relatively early phase of the import decline) the lower the observed trade reduction will be. By definition the measured duration of declines will be too short if publication delays occur. Incidentally this is not a significant factor in specifications of equation 7.1 for the depth of the import decline, but it was significant for duration and thus publication delay occurs above in the core model for duration. The *a priori* expected sign is negative ($\lambda < 0$).

Two key hypotheses will be investigated. The mainstream value chain hypothesis that is put to the test is that the occurrence of international value chains is a key driver behind both the extent and the speed of the trade collapse. One would thus expect a positive relationship of both import crunch and duration with the share of manufacturing products in total imports ($\beta > 0$ and $\xi > 0$). (Note that an alternative indicator, the share of vertical specialization in trade, will be used with the same *a priori* expected signs.)

Table 7.2   Impact of an increase of autocracy, polity and democracy scores on the depth and duration of the import crunch

	Autocracy	Relative democracy	Democracy
Depth (α)	+	−	−
Duration (θ)	−	+	+

The second hypothesis that is tested relates to the impact of trade uncertainty in different political settings. Autocracies (democracies) will move faster (slower) towards the optimal specialization point when they are confronted with an increase in trade uncertainty, so that the duration would be shorter and the depth larger. Table 7.2 lists the assumptions about the signs of the parameters to be estimated.

3. EMPIRICAL FINDINGS

Table 7.3 reports the empirical results for different specifications of the import crunch equation 7.1 and Table 7.4 does the same for the duration equation 7.2. The first column in each table reports the 'core model'. For example, the core model for import crunch reads

$$\log (import\ crunch) = -0.16 \log (import\ inclination) + \\ 0.3\log (GDP\ crunch) + constant\ term \qquad (7.1')$$

or

$$import\ crunch = constant \times import\ inclination^{-0.16} \times GDP\ crunch^{0.3} \qquad (7.1'')$$

The core model is the basic specification that does not include a variable on the characteristic decision-making institutions of the countries or the importance of international value chains. The other columns report different specifications of the model that include the variables that are used to test the hypotheses.

The econometric models in general perform satisfactorily. The core models themselves already offer a quite good description for depth and duration explaining 47 per cent and 23 per cent of the variance of the dependent variable, respectively. The estimated coefficients have the expected signs and are significant at the 99 per cent confidence level. Due to the log-linear specification, the coefficients can be directly interpreted as elasticities: an increase of GDP crunch by 1 per cent in the first specification (column 1 of Table 7.3) increases the depth of the import crunch by 0.3 per cent. Adding explanatory variables increases the explanatory power as shown by the increase of adj.-R^2 (which is R^2 adjusted for degrees of freedom).[6] As indicated by the R^2, the estimated equations explain about 50 to 60 per cent of the cross-country variation of the first dependent variable (the log of the import crunch in per cent, Table 7.3) and 39 to 45 per cent of the cross-country variation of the second dependent variable (duration in quarters, Table 7.4). This is quite comparable to other studies that econometrically investigate cross-country variations in the context of the global crisis (such as Lane and Milesi-Ferretti, 2010, regarding the variations in the changes in the rates of economic growth). The F-test is always highly significant so that the equation is significant in what it explains. The overall performance is actually quite good for this manner of research. For example, Levchenko et al. (2009) and Eichengreen and Irwin (2009) report values for R^2 below 0.2 (and often much lower).

Table 7.3   Determinants of import crunch depth in per cent (OLS, 45 countries, 2007Q1–2009Q3)

	(1)	(2)	(3)	(4)	(5)
N	42	42	42	42	34
		Democracy	Relative democracy	Democracy	Democracy
Polity		−0.04	−0.02	−0.04	−0.12
		(−1.9)	(−1.7)	(2.0)	(−3.0)
		{0.06}	{0.10}	{0.05}	{0.01}
		Share of SITC 6, 7 and 8			VSI*
log *value*		−0.37	−0.36		−0.01
chain		(−1.2)	(−1.2)		(−3.0)
indicator		{0.23}	{0.25}		{0.01}
log *import*	−0.16	−0.14	−0.15	−0.13	−0.15
inclination	(−3.0)	(−2.5)	(−2.7)	(−2.3)	(−2.8)
	{0.01}	{0.02}	{0.01}	{0.02}	{0.01}
log *GDP*	0.30	0.22	0.23	0.24	0.19
crunch	(4.0)	(2.9)	(3.0)	(3.1)	(2.2)
	{0.00}	{0.01}	{0.01}	{0.00}	{0.03}
Constant	2.4	4.4	4.3	2.9	4.0
	(16.8)	(3.5)	(3.6)	(10.2)	(8.8)
	{0.00}	{0.00}	{0.00}	{0.00}	{0.00}
R^2	0.47	0.54	0.53	0.52	0.60
Adj.-R^2	0.45	0.49	0.48	0.49	0.54
F	17.5	11.0	10.5	14.0	10.8
	{0.00}	{0.00}	{0.00}	{0.00}	{0.00}

Notes: (t value in parentheses)

{p value in brackets}

* VSI is the share of vertical specialization in trade

The findings for depth and duration agree on the significance of import inclination and the political variables (in particular the significance of the democracy indicator stands out; autocracy is only significant in the equation for duration). The estimated equations also and importantly agree that the traditional value chain argument is erroneous: if anything the importance of value chains is associated with less depth and longer duration. Let us now turn to the more detailed discussion of the findings for each independent variable.

Explaining the Depth of the Import Crunch

Columns 2–5 in Table 7.3 extend the core model by including measures that can be used to test the relevance of the value chain hypothesis and the trade uncertainty theory. These columns report different specifications of equation 7.1 so as to provide insight into the robustness of the findings. Columns 2 and 3 investigate different indicators for the political system (remember that relative democracy takes both democratic and autocratic elements into account). Column 4 leaves out the share of manufacturing trade because it is insignificant in other specifications and column 5 provides yet another test for this variable by including an alternative indicator (the share of vertical specialization in trade for which, unfortunately, fewer observations are available).

Core model and general aspects
In general the estimated equations for the depth of the import crunch perform well in a statistical sense. A sufficient part of the variance is explained. Inspection of the residuals shows a reasonable balance of underpredictions and overpredictions. The estimated equations overpredict the depth of the import crunch in Ireland, the Netherlands and Singapore (that is to say that the fitted value exceeds the actual observation). Underpredictions occur for Canada, Indonesia, South Africa and the United States. The largest prediction error occurs for South Africa, but overall the fit is sufficiently good. Also noteworthy is that the estimated parameters are quite stable across specifications. This is particularly true for the core model, where the estimated coefficients conform to *a priori* expectations and are highly significant. The estimated coefficients for the import inclination variable vary between –0.13 and –0.16 and they are significant at a confidence level of 98 per cent and better, well above the usual requirement. This finding supports the idea that countries that before the outbreak of the crisis had strongly opened up to international trade and investment (as indicated by a high import inclination ratio) will reduce their imports comparatively to a lesser extent (remember that the negative sign implies that the import crunch will be smaller for higher import inclination).

The estimated coefficients of GDP crunch vary between 0.2 and 0.3 and they are statistically significant at a confidence level of 99 per cent and better, again well above the usual requirement. Thus as expected the import crunch is larger in countries where the decrease of GDP is larger. The coefficient, although positive, is, however, also significantly smaller than 1 and thus seems to refute (at least for this crisis) the mainstream argument that imports will show stronger fluctuations than the underlying changes in final demand. This conclusion may need some further classification, because the finding may also reflect that country-specific aspects of production (that is the sector structure of the economy) may be more important for the explanation of the decline of the import volume than the overall macroeconomic demand shock. For example a country with a large durable goods industry may see a larger contraction than an economy with a large food industry. This may be a highly relevant explanation. Bems et al. (2010, p. 28, fn. 31), for example, report that '95 per cent [of disproportional increases in trade flows] is due to within-country asymmetries across sectors'.

Tests for the hypotheses

The measures for the political structures have the *a priori* expected sign and are significant at the 90 per cent level and better. In particular the democracy score is always significant at the 95 per cent confidence level and better. Inclusion of autocratic elements in the measure for political structures reduces the level of statistical significance (if I include autocracy in alternative specifications of equation 7.1, I always find the right sign but the confidence level is insufficient). The conclusion is that democracies did *ceteris paribus* reduce their import volumes to a lesser extent as predicted by the neo-classical model of trade uncertainty.

The indicators for the occurrence of international value chains have the 'wrong sign'. Contrary to the mainstream narrative value chains appear to be associated with a dampening effect on the import crunch. However, the statistical evidence does not strictly allow this conclusion.[7] While the share of vertical specialization is significant at a 94 per cent confidence level, the share of manufacturing import is never significant, so that the proper conclusion is only that the hypothesis that the presence of value chains makes the depth of the import collapse larger is refuted by the data.

So whereas the econometric investigation provides evidence that the trade uncertainty explanation may matter for the extent of the import collapse, the value chain hypothesis is not supported by the data and actually the opposite dampening effect of international value chains is more likely.

Explaining the Duration of the Import Crunch

As before, columns 2–5 in Table 7.4 extend the core model by including measures that can be used to test the relevance of the value chain hypothesis and the trade uncertainty theory (note that this analysis covers all 45 countries). These columns report different specifications of equation 7.2 so as to provide insight into the robustness of the findings.

Columns 2–4 investigate different indicators for the structure of the political system and column 5 provides as before an alternative indicator for the importance of international value chains in a country's import.

Table 7.4   *Determinants of import crunch duration in quarters (OLS, 45 countries, 2007Q1–2009Q3)*

	(1)	(2)	(3)	(4)	(5)
N	45	45	45	45	34
Polity		Autocracy	Relative democracy	Democracy	Democracy
		−0.08	0.04	0.06	0.16
		(−1.8)	(2.4)	(2.6)	(2.8)
		{0.08}	{0.02}	{0.01}	{0.01}
		Share of SITC 6, 7 and 8			VSI*
log *value chain* indicator		0.84	0.71	0.68	0.01
		(2.3)	(2.0)	(1.9)	(1.8)
		{0.03}	{0.05}	{0.07}	{0.08}
log *import inclination*	0.14	0.14	0.12	0.11	0.16
	(1.8)	(1.9)	(1.6)	(1.5)	(2.1)
	{0.07}	{0.06}	{0.12}	{0.15}	{0.04}
Publication delay (in quarters)	−0.29	−0.22	−0.17	−0.15	−0.04
	(−2.5)	(−2.0)	(−1.6)	(−1.3)	(−0.27)
	{0.01}	{0.05}	{0.12}	{0.19}	{0.79}
Constant	1.6	−1.8	−1.7	−1.7	−0.1
	(15.7)	(−1.2)	(−1.2)	(−1.2)	(−0.2)
	{0.00}	{0.23}	{0.25}	{0.23}	{0.86}
R^2	0.23	0.39	0.42	0.43	0.45
Adj.-R^2	0.20	0.33	0.37	0.38	0.38
F	6.4	6.3	7.4	7.6	5.9
	{0.00}	{0.00}	{0.00}	{0.00}	{0.00}

Notes: (t value in parentheses)

{p value in brackets}

* VSI is the share of vertical specialization in trade

Core model and general aspects

In general the estimated equations in Table 7.4 perform well in a statistical sense. A sufficient part of the variance is explained (up to 45 per cent). Inspection of the residuals shows a reasonable balance of underpredictions and overpredictions. The estimated equations overpredict the duration of the import crunch in Australia, Brazil, Germany, Indonesia, South Korea and Pakistan (so in these cases recovery occurs sooner than predicted by the model). Underpredictions occur for Italy, Malaysia and Venezuela. The largest prediction errors occur for Brazil and Malaysia. The pattern of residuals for the equation that analyses duration shows more significant prediction errors than for the depth of the import crunch, but overall the fit is still quite acceptable.

The coefficient for import inclination is again rather stable varying between 0.11 and 0.16 although it does not meet the usually required statistical significance in specifications that include an indicator that measures the extent of democracy (decentralized decision making). The positive coefficient suggests that countries that before the outbreak of the crisis had strongly opened up to international trade and investment will reduce their imports comparatively more slowly. The coefficient of the publication delay is negative as expected and this indicates that duration is not measured correctly in data sets that are not up to date (so where the end point of the data is 2009Q1 or 2009Q2 rather than 2009Q3 as for most data). The coefficient, however, is instable and sometimes completely insignificant suggesting that its significance in the first and second column is due to spurious correlation. This may be due to the fact that the group of 16 countries that produce statistics more slowly has certain characteristics that also determine duration. If so the duration variable does not reflect a measurement error or reporting problem but rather indicates the possibility for an omitted variable.

Tests for the hypotheses
In contrast to the specifications in Table 7.3 that analyse the depth of the import crunch, the signs of *all* indicators for the political structure have the *a priori* expected sign and are significant at the 90 per cent level and better (Table 7.4 columns 2–5). The negative (positive) sign for autocracy (democracy) indicates that adjustment is quicker (slower) in economies that are characterized by (de)centralized decision-making. The indicators for the occurrence of international value chains again have the 'wrong sign'. Moreover, the coefficients are significant at a 90 per cent confidence level and better in all reported specifications of equation 7.2. Contrary to the mainstream narrative, value chains appear to be associated with a dampening effect on the import crunch: duration is longer and adjustment is thus slower.

So as before the econometric investigation provides evidence that the trade uncertainty explanation may matter for the duration of the import collapse. Actually the evidence in support of the trade uncertainty explanation is quite robust since the result holds independent of the measurement of the characteristics of (de)centralized decision making. We should remember that this is an indirect relationship and that further research on this topic is needed. The mainstream value chain hypothesis is refuted by the data.

Evaluation of the Two Estimated Equations

All in all the estimated equations agree on the impact of a number of drivers of both aspects of the import volume crunch during the period 2007–2009Q3. Both the depth and the duration of the contraction are less serious in decentralized (democratic) economies and in economies that had opened up more strongly before the outbreak of the crisis. The empirical investigation did not produce evidence that supports the mainstream hypothesis that the occurrence and intensity of international value chains caused the import collapse in the import volume of the 45 countries studied in this chapter.

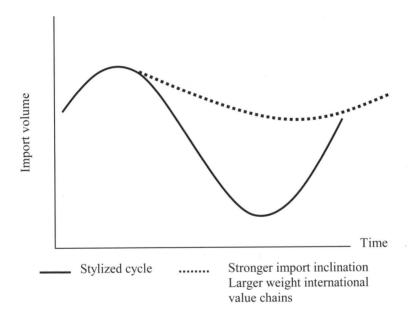

—— Stylized cycle   ⋯⋯⋯   Stronger import inclination
                              Larger weight international
                              value chains

Figure 7.1   Stylized cycle and the impact of decentralized decision-making, stronger import inclination and/or larger weight of international value chains

It is also possible to combine the insights from the two sets of estimates in Tables 7.3 and 7.4 in order to get an idea of what this means for the different trajectories that can be discerned for different country attributes. Both for a country's import inclination, for decentralized decision-making and for the share of international value chain activities in its trade flows we find a positive correlation with duration and a negative correlation with the depth of the import crunch. Thus more open, decentralized (democratic) countries for which international value chains make up a larger part of import activity will have smaller depth of the import crunch and a longer period of contraction.

As illustrated by the dotted line in Figure 7.1, countries with these characteristics will trade more than the sample average over the initial phase of the trade cycle. The figure suggests the existence of a trade-off between, on the one hand, a strategy of abrupt and swift adjustment that may lead to a fast recovery and, on the other hand, a strategy of slower adjustment. The volume of imports in the former strategy starts to exceed that of the latter at the point of intersection of the stylized cycle and the dotted line. However, the loss of trade up until that point is larger in the quick-adjustment strategy. (Note that the observed cyclical pattern may alternatively reflect the time path of an economy that adjusts to a new regime of higher trade uncertainty, as discussed in the previous chapter and illustrated in Figure 6.4.)

4.   DISCUSSION AND CONCLUSIONS

Clearly these results are not beyond scientific doubt, both due to data deficiencies and because the approach is not based on a theoretical model but rather quasi-postulates a reduced form equation. This implies that additional sensitivity testing should be considered regarding the specification. Sensitivity testing does of course not solve the problem of a lacking formal theoretical structure. It is not a sufficient condition for scientific acceptance of the empirical findings and my interpretation of the results, but it is a necessary condition. So before we can draw conclusions we need to consider this question: are the results sensitive to specification of the equation and the way the explanatory variables have been defined?

Sensitivity Analyses

The first issue to consider is the functional form of the estimated reduced form equation. Thus all specifications of equations 7.1 and 7.2 were also estimated in linear form. The results of this exercise were quite comparable because both the explanatory power was not reduced for the linear specifications and the signs of the estimated coefficients did not change while their statistical significance was more or less in line with the findings for the log-linear specifications.[8] The noteworthy differences in this sensitivity analysis can be summarized as follows. Firstly, the variables that describe the political structure (the decision-making characteristics) are for the estimated versions of equation 7.1 highly significant at the 99 per cent confidence level (the 'worst' result in the linear specification is for autocracy that is significant at the 93 per cent confidence level). Secondly, the share of manufacturing trade is completely insignificant in the linear versions of both equations 7.1 and 7.2. The share of vertical specialization in trade remains highly significant in equation 7.1 but is insignificant in equation 7.2. The impact on the significance level of import inclination varies: it deteriorates substantially in equation 7.1 and often turns out to be just below the 90 per cent bench mark, but in contrast it is now always significant in equation 7.2 at a confidence level of at least 93 per cent. The conclusion of this part of the sensitivity analysis is that the results are from my perspective sufficiently robust. Indeed, the alternative linear approach offers somewhat stronger evidence for the political variables and stronger evidence against the main-stream definition of the value chain hypothesis. Only the interpretation of the findings on import inclination that are reported in Tables 7.3 and 7.4 is less straightforward and needs some nuance.

A second approach to get an idea of the robustness of the results is to use different measures of variables with which to test key hypotheses, to see what happens for different subsets of the data and to include other potentially relevant explanatory variables and to see how this changes the significance levels of the new measures and the other variables in the equations. The first thing to note is that Tables 7.3 and 7.4 analyse different definitions of the seriousness of the trade collapse, namely depth and duration of the decline in import volumes, and reach basically the same conclusions about the two key hypotheses that have been put to the test. The second thing to note is that Tables 7.3 and 7.4 also report different measures for the political variables and value chain indicators and the sample changes already due to these sensitivity analyses (and as said before these results hold for the alternative linear specifications).[9] In addition to these sensitivity analyses that already imply substantial robustness of the results it is worth reporting that the equation for duration was also estimated for the sample of 42 countries (to which columns 2–4 in Table 7.3 relate). Moreover, a test was performed to check for differences for countries for which the trough had not yet been identified (so where the growth rate of the volume of imports had not yet turned positive and where the import crunch thus at the end of 2009Q3 had to be identified as potentially ongoing). The ongoing character of the trade adjustment was not significant for the duration (equation 7.2) but it was sometimes significant and positive with respect to the percentage decline of imports. Also in these specifications, however, the overall empirical results did not change. Coefficients and significance levels remained at the same level. All in all the estimated equations perform satisfactorily in a statistical sense and provide robust empirical results.

Summing Up

The preliminary cross-country investigation of competing theories regarding the drivers of the trade collapse in individual countries provides a few clues why individual country experience during the trade collapse differed so much. Countries that before the crisis had opened up strongly to international trade and investment (as indicated by a high import inclination ratio) reduced their imports comparatively to a lesser extent. Countries with large shares of manufactures in trade (a proxy for international value chain activity) did not reduce their trade more strongly than countries that relied more on trade in for example agricultural goods and natural resources and the empirical evidence actually points out that international value chains very well could have been a major dampening cause that reduced the extent to which trade fell.

It is especially relevant that the measure for the extent of (de)centralized decision making is significant and not only because this provides an indirect test of the trade uncertainty hypothesis. To put it simply: democracies according to the econometric analysis react too late and too slowly and, consequently, trade too much for their own good – their decentralized reaction to trade uncertainty is suboptimal. For small open democracies this finding would seem to suggest that trade needs to be reduced to some extent and this do-it-yourself policy advice brings me to the final chapter of this book: the policy advice that has been given and in particular the role of the professional economist in designing economic policies to meet the challenge of deglobalization.

NOTES

[1] Exchange rate variability can of course become a substantial barrier to trade, but that is not the WTO's point.

[2] Note that this variable is a crude measure of the potential presence of value chains and does not reflect the intensity and extent of fragmentation *per se*.

[3] The Standard International Trade Classification (SITC) is used to classify internationally traded goods. SITC 6 comprises Manufactured goods classified chiefly by material, SITC 7 comprises Machinery and transport equipment and SITC8 Miscellaneous manufactured articles, see the website of the UN Statistical Division for the detailed (sub-level) structure and explanatory notes at http://unstats.un.org/unsd/cr/registry/regcst.asp?Cl=14&Lg=1&Top=1.

4 Frankel et al. (1996) follow the same approach (although in the context of economic growth models) identifying policies for outward orientation by means of the fact that trade shares predicted by a gravity model exceed the observed trade shares.

5 Note that this is a rather strong assumption. Statistically speaking one would expect a mean reversal tendency pushing trade to return to the level predicted by the model. So in the case of strong import inclination (actual observed import exceeds the in-sample prediction) one would statistically expect a *stronger* reduction of imports. The empirical finding that such countries actual reduce imports to a *lesser* extent thus carries extra weight. In the same vein an insignificant coefficient for import inclination still points out the existence of a countervailing power along the lines discussed in the main text.

6 This is supported by formal F tests on restricted models (the core models) versus extended models that also include political variables and the indicators for the importance of international value chain. Note also that the wish to increase the number of explanatory variables sometimes reduces the available number of observations somewhat due to lacking data. All reported results and comparisons are also valid when we restrict the sample from the start to those countries for which all data are available.

7 Escaith et al. (2010) find that the heterogeneity in country experiences cannot be explained by vertical specialization.

8 Actually R^2, adj.-R^2 and F test are a bit better for the linear specifications.

9 In van Bergeijk (2009c) I also check alternative specification with and without import inclination (also because import inclination and the extent of decentralized decision making may be correlated) and do not find a measurable impact on the significance levels of the political variables.

Appendix 7A.1: Data Sources

This appendix describes the data sources that have been used in the empirical investigations. Table 7A.1 lists the 45 countries included in the analysis.

Data on the Import Volume and GDP

Import crunch in per cent is measured peak to trough over 2007Q4–2009Q3 from two sources (in brackets latest available observation if not 2009Q3). Duration is measured in quarters using the same data and method.

OECD National Accounts

The data are seasonally adjusted and available for: Australia (2009Q2), Austria, Belgium, Canada, Chile, Czech Republic (2009Q2), Denmark (2009Q2), Finland, France, Germany, Greece, Hungary, Ireland, Israel, Italy, Japan, Korea (South), Mexico (2009Q2), Netherlands, New Zealand (2009Q2), Norway, Poland, Portugal, Russia (2009Q2), Spain, Sweden, Switzerland, Thailand, Turkey, UK, USA.

IMF International Financial Statistics
(a) Import volume seasonally adjusted: Ecuador, Pakistan (2009Q1), Singapore , Thailand.
(b) National Accounts data deflated by GDP deflator: Argentina (2009Q2), Belarus (2009Q2), Bulgaria (2009Q2), India (2009Q2), Indonesia, Malaysia (2009Q2), Peru (2009Q2), Romania (2009Q2), South Africa (2009Q2)
(c) National Accounts data deflated by import wholesale price index: Venezuela (2009Q2).

GDP

In order to ensure consistency, GDP data have been derived from the same sources as the import volumes. Quarterly data were not available for Pakistan and Ecuador.

International Value Chains

Two measures are included to analyse the impact of the presence of international value chains

Manufacturing trade

Manufacturing share is measured as the share of the categories SITC 6, 7 and 8 in total imports (in per cent and for the year 2007) and derived from United Nations, 2008, *International Merchandise Trade Statistics Yearbook Volume II country pages*, UN: Geneva and New York.

Share of vertical specialization

Data on the share of vertical specialization are for the most recent year (most often 2005) and derived from OECD 2009d, Table 1.

Import Inclination

I derive observed and predicted bilateral imports from a gravity model estimated for the year 2006 and 63 countries (Yakop and van Bergeijk 2009). Table 7A.1 lists import inclination ratios for the 45 countries included in this research.

The gravity model is an applied empirical trade model that describes bilateral trade flows. The key drivers in this model are economic mass and distance. Just as in the Newtonian gravity model this trade model assumes that interaction is weaker if distance is larger and stronger when masses are larger. Thus a large country that has substantial production and population will *ceteris paribus* trade more than a small country. Likewise countries that are closer to each other trade more. Often the model also includes a great number of trade resistance factors (such as import tariffs) and trade enhancement factors (such as a common language) that are relevant at the bilateral level.

The gravity model is one of the most robust and widely used tools of applied trade analysis. Notably, it has done an excellent job in situations that were characterized by significant structural change in global trade flows such as during the 1990s when the Iron Curtain fell (van Bergeijk and Brakman 2010).

Table 7A.1   Import inclination (45 countries, 2006)

Country	Import inclination	Country	Import inclination
Argentina	0.20	Korea South	0.31
Australia	0.15	Malaysia	0.08
Austria	0.39	Mexico	0.67
Belarus	0.40	Netherlands	0.56
Belgium	0.84	New Zealand	0.12
Brazil	0.39	Norway	0.40
Bulgaria	0.14	Pakistan	0.46
Canada	1.93	Peru	0.22
Chile	0.16	Poland	0.46
Czech Republic	0.27	Portugal	0.27
Denmark	0.58	Romania	0.20
Ecuador	0.17	Russia	0.30
Finland	0.20	Singapore	0.11
France	1.28	South Africa	0.18
Germany	1.12	Spain	0.46
Greece	0.39	Sweden	0.25
Hungary	0.16	Switzerland	1.21
India	0.74	Thailand	0.09
Indonesia	0.24	Turkey	0.27
Ireland	0.56	UK	0.82
Israel	0.41	United States	2.68
Italy	0.61	Venezuela	0.29
Japan	0.50		

Democracy and Autocracy

The Polity IV dataset (http://www.systemicpeace.org/polity/polity4.htm) is used to describe the political system of the economy. Polity IV as its predecessor Polity III (Jaggers and Gurr, 1995) contains operational indicators of institutionalized authority characteristics. Polity IV annually codes nine democracy and autocracy indicators for 162 countries (all independent countries that in the early 1990s had a population greater than 500,000).

Table 7A.2 illustrates which elements play a role in the coding. Aggregating these elements yields the 'autocracy score' and the 'democracy score' for a specific country in a specific year. Subtracting the autocracy score from the democracy score yields a summary measure ('relative democracy').

Table 7A.2 The construction of democracy and autocracy indicators in the Polity data set

Authority coding	Democracy score	Autocracy score
Competitiveness of political participation		
a) Competitive	3	0
b) Transitional	2	0
c) Factional	1	0
d) Restricted	0	1
e) Suppressed	0	2
Regulation of political participation		
a) Factional/restricted	0	1
b) Restricted	0	2
Competitiveness of executive recruitment		
a) Election	2	0
b) Transitional	1	0
c) Selection	0	2
Openness of executive recruitment		
a) Election	1	0
b) Dual: hereditary/election	1	0
c) Dual: hereditary/designation	0	1
d) Closed	0	1
Constraints on chief executive		
a) Executive parity or subordination	4	0
b) Intermediate	3	0
c) Substantial limitations	2	0
d) Intermediate	1	0
e) Slight to moderate limitations	0	1
f) Intermediate	0	2
g) Unlimited power of the executive	0	3

Source: Jaggers and Gurr (1995), p. 472

Many empirical measures for political regimes have already been designed and applied by political scientists. Since economists are no experts on measuring 'democracy', it is important that the conceptual and empirical foundations of the data set that we use in our analysis are scientifically valid. Jaggers and Gurr (1995) compared the validity of Polity III's coding of regime types with seven conceptually and operationally different indicators developed by other political scientists. They find strong correlations (0.85 to 0.92) between Polity III and the other seven data sets, so that it seems safe to conclude that the Polity indicators describe 'democracy' and 'autocracy' satisfactorily.

The data for autocracy, democracy and relative democracy are all for 2007.

8. Too Early to Tell?

Should economists have refrained from policy advice during the early phase of the world trade collapse? This question arises because many professional economists in the early downward phase of the trade cycle provided strong policy advice: support trade credit, count on a quick mean-reversing rebound of cross-border economic activity, reduce reliance on foreign trade and in particular on international value chain activities, and be aware of protectionism all around the world. Policy makers and politicians took the economists seriously and were keen to follow up on this advice. Many issues were taken up in the context of G20 meetings. This should not have come as a surprise, after all the policy prescriptions looked like very sensible and coherence advice. With hindsight that advice, however, appears to have been based on shaky grounds and, moreover, incomplete.

The main suspects in the dominant world trade collapse narrative – trade finance, international value chains and protectionism – have probably been innocent eyewitnesses. Firstly, the trade credit collapse appears to have been the consequence of the world trade collapse rather than its cause. Chapter 3 showed that world trade contracted before trade finance (activity) started to decrease. We also saw that publicly supplied funds exceeded demand by substantial amounts, which is the more telling since public funds may very well have driven out the private sector suppliers of trade finance. Anyhow, in a situation where supply exceeds demand, it is not likely that the main problem is on the supply side. Secondly, international value chains probably were supporting global trade as suggested by the econometric findings in Chapter 7. At a minimum the presence of global value chains appears not to have been associated with the strength and speed of the decline of trade flows, but (as we discussed in Chapter 4) may have provided leeway building on the kind of mutual trust that develops in long-run trading relationships. Thirdly, the level of protectionism was rather low at the start of the downturn in global trade as discussed in Chapter 5 although the risk is clear that this may change in the near future (for example, when the measures in the pipeline are actually implemented as this may increase the observed level by a factor of 3 to 5). The analysis on which the mainstream narrative was constructed was also incomplete, as discussed in Chapter 6, because one of the driving forces of the world trade collapse (the increase in perceived trade uncertainty) was not explicitly recognized in the analysis and insufficiently addressed in policy advice.

With hindsight the early 2009 narrative of the world trade collapse should therefore have been different and policy should at least have tackled the trade uncertainty externality, recognizing the importance of the global networks of businesses that cooperate in international value chains.

Early 2009 policy advice was not only influential and effective in shaping the agenda for the G20; it also misdirected both scarce resources and the attention of policy makers. This implies first of all a waste of scarce resources as a lot of energy was probably put in the wrong (or at least 'suboptimal') kind of policy initiatives. The substantial amounts of public sector support for trade credit could, for example, in all likelihood have been used better (for example, in order to support development aid commitments), crowded out private banking activity (which is particularly relevant in view of the relatively low risk character of this activity) and – most importantly – allowed politicians to present themselves as being actively involved, thus concealing their lack of commitment to the real solutions. It is very likely that both the global benefits of a completion of the Doha Round of multilateral trade negotiations and the costs of trade finance initiatives, policies that aimed at reducing openness and advice that put a low weight on cooperation with foreign firms, were underestimated. So perhaps economists have been simply too eager to provide policy advice. It was too early to tell the story that became the main narrative for the causes of the trade collapse in 2009.

But could economists actually have refrained from policy advice as soon as the world trade collapse became apparent? Or did the profession have no other choice but to provide its views in an early phase? After all such perspectives on a unique and potentially very destabilizing development may have been inaccurate, but they were probably also indispensible for policy makers. And would it not have been unacceptable if economic advice was not provided in times that policy makers and politicians needed guidance?

Three Points to Reconsider

Of course one has to accept the criticism that the best horseman always stands on his feet and to acknowledge that it is easy and often too easy to criticize analyses and advice that were provided in the midst of crisis. This being said, however, one cannot but get the impression that advice was provided on topics for which theoretical prejudice rather than actual observations formed the basis. In itself this is not problematic, but the fact that policy advice was probably counterproductive does provide food for thought for many in the profession. In particular three aspects need reconsideration:

- it should have been recognized from the start that the necessary data were not available to test the potential explanations for the world trade collapse and this should have cautioned against too strong an advice in a specific direction;
- observations, simulations and econometric estimates that did not make sense from the perspective of the dominant narrative were all too often discarded whereas such findings should have been highlighted in order to both stimulate research in different directions and clarify the imprecision of the knowledge base to the users of policy analysis; and
- the narrative that developed in the early phase of the trade collapse was uncritically accepted and it even developed in some sort of mantra that was recited in international economic analysis and advice but hardly ever checked.

My discomfort with the profession's analysis and advice is, however, not only related to the early analysis of the world trade collapse. I am also unhappy with the fact that the tone of the advice often turned against strategies that opt for international specialization and undisturbed international trade and investment. This will be the topic of Section 1 which discusses some influential specimen of policy advice that increases the risk of moving the world economy into the direction of deglobalization. Section 2 concentrates on four second round effects of a reduction in the level of openness that are not always appreciated or considered in the studies that were discussed in this book, in particular its impact on long-run growth, the co-movement of economies, specialization patterns and non-economic issue areas in international politics. Section 3 gives some thoughts on the new narrative that is needed for the explanation of the world trade collapse. This new narrative will not only be needed in case of a prolonged trade recession. It is equally necessary if the world economy shows positive and sustainable growth rates for real trade and investment flows in 2010, because it will influence future policy responses.

1. PROTECTIONISM AND THE INTELLECTUAL

In times of severe crisis purely national interests gain the upper hand and often policy advisors propose protectionist measures. Especially (the threat of) high unemployment is a powerful incentive to reduce imports by means of tariffs and non-tariff barriers such as quotas and regulations. Even economists that under normal conditions are pro free trade advisors may find themselves in a position where they have to compromise between the 'theoretically optimal' and the 'practically possible'. For example, in the 1930s both

Keynes and Tinbergen accepted the need to consider import barriers as appropriate second-best instruments to fight the depression – at least for some countries. Keynes was especially outspoken although his theoretical position can at least partly be explained by the fact that he was assuming that the Gold Standard would be continued. Once Britain was off gold Keynes changed his view and advised again against protectionism. But the explanation is only partial because Keynes was never willing to give up this instrument as he assumed that some sort of control over trade flows would be necessary in the international institutional framework that was to be created after the Second World War (see Kindleberger 1973 and Eichengreen 1984).

Keynes's intellectual position in the wake of critical economic developments is by no means a unique phenomenon. It is characteristic for periods of deglobalization and depression that import substitution is seen as a viable alternative in policy quarters. During the world trade collapse even those international institutions that are assumed to underpin the open world economic system fell into this trap of second-best de-internationalization. An example is the IMF's 2009 Article IV Consultation of China. Actually the Executive Board

> supported the steps that China is taking to bolster private consumption as part of a comprehensive, well-sequenced strategy aimed at rebalancing China's growth model, and saw further room for policies *to reduce China's dependence on exports and high levels of investment* (IMF 2009c, emphasis added).

Another example is Rodrik (2009) who discusses the impact of the crisis on developing countries. Rodrik argues that the fast growth of the emerging markets (Japan, the Asian Tigers, Eastern Europe, the BRIIC countries, etc.) in the past 50 years was possible due to the fact that these countries captured growing shares of the world market for non-primary products – a development strategy that according to Rodrik is no longer feasible for large and middle income economies as the financial crisis will probably limit the US's ability to run large trade deficits. Accordingly he proposes industrial policies as a panacea: that is to increase the profitability of these products by tax exemptions, direct credit, payroll subsidies, investment subsidies etc. There is only one important obstacle, namely the WTO:

> In a world where economic growth requires the encouragement of modern economic activities in developing nations, the Agreement on Subsidies makes little economic sense (Rodrik 2009, p. 24).

I disagree. The WTO rules and procedures are essential for the future course of both developing countries and the industrialized world. My argument is of course not that the neoclassical free trade recipe is sacred. My point is basically that a global shock in trade uncertainty appears to have been one of the key factors behind the trade collapse. So far policy makers have avoided the error of the 1930s to rely on trade barriers and other beggar-thy-neighbour policies. Although there are some early signs of stabilization of world trade at the start of 2010, the situation would still seem to be extremely fragile. First-best government action therefore should be aimed at reducing uncertainty *per se* through strict adherence to conflict settlement procedures. Indeed, such policies tackle uncertainty externalities directly. It may be especially relevant for small and medium-sized economies as the WTO seeks to protect their interests in open and multilateral trade against the (market) power of the large economies. The world does not need pleas that in the end lead economies to de-specialize and unwind their interaction with other countries.

2. THE SECOND ROUND

The previous section already provided some sobering observations on 'deglobalization advice', but in addition it is relevant to consider four second-order effects that are implied by the reductions in world trade and the reflux in openness of the international system. Openness to international trade and investment often has effects that go beyond narrowly defined areas of investigation that are characteristic of modern economic research agendas. These feedback mechanisms could induce a second phase of world trade collapse or prolong a period of world trade stagnation. Such second round effects may take some years before they actually materialize and should thus be analysed in addition to the short-run movements that were studied in Chapter 7. This section discusses the four main feedbacks that relate to long-run growth, the co-movement of economies, trade policy feedbacks and non-economic issue areas where reduced cooperation among countries and even an increasing risk of international conflict can be expected.

Long Run Growth

The reduction of multilateral trade openness will in all likelihood exert a negative impact on long-run growth of production and trade.[1] A reduction in levels of openness implies less competition, less exchange of technology and fewer scale economies and thus lower factor productivity growth. This would seem to reflect a consensus view that can be distilled from the econometric literature on trade and growth. Lewer and van den Berg (2003) provide a meta-analysis that analyses 246 cross-section regressions and 596 time-series regressions that were reported in 83 econometric studies published in scientific journals over the years 1960–2002. On the basis of the point estimates the studies yield a consensus view that a 1 percentage point reduction in the growth rate of the volume of exports on average decreases annual real long-run GDP growth by 0.2 percentage points.

Based on our discussion in Chapter 1 it seems not unreasonable to expect a reduction in the world trade-to-GDP ratio by 3 percentage points and a negative growth rate for world trade in excess of 10 per cent. These declines could induce strong second-round effects. According to simulations with the computable general equilibrium model MIRAGE (Bénassy-Quéré et al., 2009) a halt to the globalization trend reduces the rate of growth for the volume of world trade by 2 percentage points while a reversal of previous trends (that is actual 'deglobalization') could induce another decline in this order of magnitude.[2] Lower multilateral trade openness will thus further reduce the scope for a recovery from the financial crisis and the concomitant world trade collapse.

Co-movement and Stability

The trade channel is often seen as feeding and transmitting instability across countries. The *a priori* argument is as convincing as it is irrelevant. Autarkic countries would be isolated from what happens in the rest of the world in the same sense as economic activity on Mars is not influenced by Earth's business cycle. Such completely isolated economies hardly exist and the relevant issue is of course one of gradation. Is it wise to depend to a lesser or to a larger extent on economic activities in other countries? We have seen that one negative connotation of the mainstream value chain hypothesis is its suggestion that the fluctuations in international business-to-business networks are presently injecting more instability into national economies due to changes in the structure and geography of world trade flows since the mid 1990s. This would seem to suggest that the linkages between economies carry an increasingly large cost in terms of stronger fluctuations and thus clear the ground for policy advice aimed at less economic linkage.

The findings in this book, however, suggest that openness also had dampening effects. Larger value chain activity, according to Chapter 7, is associated with a smaller decline in the volume of imports, and countries that had opened up their economies more strongly had smaller reductions in import volumes. This dampening effect is a relevant although as yet not fully recognized issue, in particular regarding the empirical context of the most recent developments (that is including observations that relate to 2007, 2008 and 2009). Other observers also suggest that international openness has had dampening effects that counteracted co-movements of economies. An example is an IMF analysis of the role of linkages in determining the extent of co-movement of economic stress in emerging economies during the crisis

(IMF 2009a, pp. 154–60). Distinguishing between periods of international stress and calmness, one finding of the IMF is that trade linkages showed a meaningful correlation prior to 2007, but do not appear to have significantly influenced the spread of stress in the period after July 2007 (IMF 2009a, Table 4.2, p. 158). Moreover, financial stress in emerging markets is significantly lower for open economies in equations that take country-specific effects into account: 'trade openness (...) reduces the level of financial stress' (IMF 2009a, p. 159).

The upshot is that such dampening second order effects will be reduced in a less open world economy. A lack of such cushioning effects makes the world more vulnerable for shocks as weaker counteracting forces will also tend to reduce the stability of the market equilibrium.

Specialization Patterns and Trade Policy Feedbacks

The financial crisis could induce economic nationalism, protectionism and a flight into import substitution activities especially if the recovery is protracted and erratic as it was in the 1930s. Nationalism, as we saw in Chapter 5, correlates at the level of individual preferences with protectionist trade policy preferences. Another relevant observation in Chapter 5 was the existence of a substantial amount of protectionist trade policy measures hanging above the market in early 2010. Also from this point of view the experience of the 1930s is relevant in that the decline of world trade induced substantial increases in protectionism, especially in those countries that had no alternative policy instruments available (or at least believed they had no alternative in the policy mix that they considered appropriate). The third trade policy feedback element to consider is the move towards import substitution that is explicitly advised as we saw in the previous section. Import substitution reduces the efficiency of the economy: import substitution strategies have often failed to deliver what they promised, protecting and fossilizing industries that could not compete on the world market and detracting resources from those industries that could meet international economic rivalry. This is of course detrimental to the economy that implements such policies, but also its trade partners will be influenced because their trade opportunities are reduced.

All in all the world trade collapse can be expected to have increased perceptions of future trade uncertainty. Importantly, even without concrete and observable trade conflicts a perception of increased uncertainty about future trading possibilities can already change the intensity and pattern of international specialization as we discussed in Chapter 6.

On the Brink of Deglobalization

Conflict and Cooperation

One of the issues that motivated many people involved in the 1944 Bretton Woods conference that resulted in the international economic institutions that we know today was to prevent the re-emergence of world war. Unfortunately it is not unlikely that non-economic second-round effects of the world trade collapse may occur in the field of international politics. A rich empirical literature exists of studies that deal with the trade–conflict relationship (that is: how do changes in the level of international trade and investment influence levels of both conflict and co-operation between nations) and the conflict–trade relationship (that is the mirror question of how political conflicts hinder international trade or how the reduction of conflict increases trade) (see van Bergeijk 2009a, Chapter 2). Although the causality issue has not been settled yet in international economics and political science, little dispute exists about the significantly negative relation between the two variables.[3]

Table 8.1 Meta-analysis of 15 empirical studies published in the years 1980–2006 on the trade–conflict nexus (dependent variable: reported trade–conflict elasticity)

Publication lag (years passed between publication and latest data point) [a]	-0.03^{*}
	(-1.92)
Dataset pre 1980	-0.25^{*}
	(-2.11)
Assumed direction of causality (dummy) [b]	0.11
	(1.78)
Terrorism	0.27^{***}
	(3.04)
R^2	0.59
F test	3.6^{**}

Source: van Bergeijk (2009d)

Notes: [a] year of publication minus last year of estimation period
 [b] dummy = 0 for impact of conflict on trade
 *** significant at 99%
 ** significant at 95%
 * significant at 90%
 (t values in brackets)
 The constant term is negative and significant but not reported

This is illustrated in Table 8.1 that reports on a meta-analysis of 15 scientific studies that were published in the years 1980–2006. Typically, a meta-analysis combines the results of several studies that address a set of related research hypotheses. Usually this is done by means of the identification of a common measure or effect size, which is modelled using a form of meta-regression (in this case straightforward Ordinary Least Squares). The meta-analysis in Table 8.1 controls for three study characteristics: publication lag (that is the 'age' of the data sources at the time of the analysis and the year of publication of that data set), the type of conflict (terrorism versus other conflicts) and the direction of causality. The meta-effect size is a more powerful estimate of the true effect size than the effect reports in a single study under a given single set of assumptions and conditions and on average amounts to an elasticity of −0.22.[4] The meta-effect in these 15 studies suggests that an increase in the level of international conflict could result alongside the world trade collapse. The empirical regularity that lower levels of bilateral trade are associated with higher levels of conflict between nations is actually an important argument for the industrialized world to increase the international economic relationships with China and other emerging economies.

All in all one does not need to be a Dr Doom to be concerned about potential second round effects in the aftermath of the 2009 trade collapse. These second round effects could occur as we saw in a great many fields. It is too early to say anything meaningful in a scientific manner and the next section is therefore by necessity speculative.

3. IN SEARCH OF THE NEW NARRATIVE

Is the world trade collapse a break in the internationalization process or just an incident with a large but also transient impact? We will probably need another decade or so to get the perspective on the world trade collapse right, as incidentally has always been the case with the major shocks in the world economic system. The world trade collapse may have been a symptom of a fundamental change in the division of economic power, it may have reflected growing and unsustainable current account imbalances or it could have been the consequence of increasing complexity of the international networks of nations and firms. Or it could have been an extreme case of bad luck.

The findings in this book showed for individual cases that a financial crisis in general exerts a strong and negative impact on the volume of imports. The concurrence of financial crises in a great many countries during the two world trade collapses that we studied implies that global import demand will contract so that an export led recovery is difficult to conceive for individual countries and for the world as a whole for that matter. The reader would be ill-advised if she was to rely on an automatic mean-reversal tendency in the volume of world trade and investment. Several authors would seem to agree as they have pointed out that 'this time it is different'. Robertson (2009) draws attention to the fact that the shock to international trade has been historically strong and argues that this increases the likelihood that path dependence or hysteresis will keep economies for long from the *status quo ante* so that substantially reduced levels of international specialization and dependence on international trade and investment could be characteristic for the 2010s, just as they were for the 1930s. Escaith (2009, p. 9) points out the fact that reactivation of disturbed international value chains will be gradual at best. In this sense the average duration of the financial crises that have been studied in Chapter 2 should best be considered as a lower bound estimate for the duration of the world trade collapse.

In 2010 the world is poised on the brink of deglobalization. If the world is lucky the world economic system will recover quickly, but that is not going to happen automatically and will require positive policy action. The interpretation of the world trade collapse that forms the basis for the mainstream narrative that this book critically evaluated, needs to be revised in order to see where positive policy action would have to be developed. The explanation of the world trade collapse should acknowledge the following elements.

- The key feature of the world trade collapse in 2009 is the shock in perceived trade uncertainty which induced lower levels of international specialization.
- During the crisis international economic exchange and specialization continued to play their positive role in the world economy. The presence of international value chains did not strengthen the trade collapse and probably has dampened it.
- Concurrence of trade shocks (that is the global nature of the world trade collapse) is an important element regarding both the depth and duration of the trade contraction.
- Capital flows played an important role, but not so much because the financing of trade dried up. Rather the driving force was the contraction of foreign direct investment which may have dampened the trade collapse and may exert its influence over longer periods of time.
- The crisis in world trade was not caused by protectionism.

It is impossible to foresee which course world trade will take in 2010 and beyond. Undoubtedly some of the above elements will have to be reconsidered, for example if trade were to follow a W-shaped pattern (because in that case the developments that were analysed in this book would be 'unfinished') or alternatively if full recovery were to occur in an unexpectedly short period. The narrative of the downturn would probably also have to be adapted if the potential second-round effects actually materialized, for example, if protectionism were to revive as a consequence of the trade collapse in 2009. So the narrative that I suggest will also be criticized and amended, but I doubt that much will change regarding the first three listed elements: the importance of trade uncertainty, the positive role of international exchange and the fact that almost all countries are in trouble. These elements provide the argument to strive for greater security for trade and to support all efforts to strengthen the open multilateral trading system, guided by WTO rules as a clear commitment to free trade.

I end this book with an appropriate *ceterum censeo*: the conclusion of the Doha Round would show a clear commitment for multilateral negotiations and provide a much needed antidote against protectionism, trade uncertainty and global instability.

NOTES

[1] Note that this argument is about the long-run rate of growth, not about the short-term rate which could be high once trade and production hit sustainable bottoms in 2010.

[2] This would amount to roughly half the simulated world trade reduction in MIRAGE (Bénassy-Quéré et al. 2009, p. 27).

[3] Note, however, that the strength of the estimated effect tends to be smaller in more recent datasets.

[4] The detailed results of this meta-analysis can be summarized as follows. Almost 60 per cent of the variation of the estimated coefficients can be explained by a simple regression. It matters whether the dataset that is used in the study is less recent (either from the perspective of the time lapse between the end-year of the data set and the year of publication or in the sense that the study deals only with periods prior to 1980) as the relationship appears weaker for the more recent past. Also the particular form of conflict matters: studies that deal with terrorism find a smaller effect. The assumed causality is not a significant determinant of the reported elasticity so that the studies that have been included in the meta-analysis agree on the strength of the mechanism even when they disagree on the assumed causality.

References

Afman, E.R. and M. Maurel, 2010, 'Diplomatic relations and trade reorientation in transition countries', in: P.A.G. van Bergeijk and S. Brakman (eds), 2010, *The Gravity Model in International Trade: Advances and Applications*, Cambridge University Press: Cambridge, pp. 278–95.

Aidt, T.S. and M. Gassebner, 2007, 'Do Autocratic States Trade Less?', *KOF Working Papers 175*, ETH: Zürich.

Amador, J. and S. Cabral, 2009, 'Vertical specialization around the world: a relative measure', *North American Journal of Economics and Finance*, **20**, pp. 267–80.

Anderson, J.E. and J.P. Neary, 2005, *Measuring the Restrictiveness of International Trade Policy*, The MIT Press: Cambridge MA.

Araújo, S. and J. Oliveira Martins, 2009, 'The great synchronisation: what do high-frequency statistics tell us about the trade collapse?', *Vox* (www.voxeu.org), July 8.

Arribas, I, F. Pérez and E. Tortosa-Ausina, 2009, 'Measuring globalization of international trade: theory and evidence', *World Development*, **27** (1), pp. 127–45.

Auboin, M., 2009a, 'Trade finance: G20 and follow-up', *Vox* (www.voxeu.org), June 5, 2009.

Auboin, M., 2009b, 'Restoring Trade Finance During a Period of Financial Crisis: Stock-taking of Recent Initiatives', *WTO Staff Working Paper ERSD-2009-16*, WTO: Geneva.

Auboin, M. and M. Meier-Ewert, 2003, 'Improving the Availability of Trade Finance during Financial Crises', *WTO Discussion Paper*, WTO: Geneva.

Awati, M. and D.E. Weinstein, 2009, 'Exports and Financial Shocks', *NBER Working Paper No. 15556*, NBER: Cambridge MA.

Baldwin, R.E. and S.J. Evenett, 2009, *The Collapse of Global Trade, Murky Protectionism, and the Crisis: Recommendations for the G20*, A Vox EU publication: London.

Bems, R., R.C. Johnson and K.-M. Yi, 2010, 'The Role of Vertical Linkages in the Propagation of the Global Downturn of 2008', paper presented at 'Economic Linkages, Spillovers and the Financial Crisis', Paris, January 29, 2010.

Bénassy-Quéré, A., Y. Decreux, L. Fontagné and D. Khoudour-Casteras, 2009, 'Economic Crisis and Global Supply Chains', *CEPII Document du travail 2009 – 15*, CEPII: Paris.

Bergeijk, P.A.G. van, 1995, 'The accuracy of international economic observations', *Bulletin of Economic Research*, **47** (1), pp. 1–20.

Bergeijk, P.A.G. van, 1999, Systeemschokken: Staat de econoom echt met lege handen?' (Systemic shocks: is the economist really unable to say anything meaningful?', in Dutch), Inaugural address, Erasmus University: Rotterdam.

Bergeijk, P.A.G. van, 2009a, *Economic Diplomacy and the Geography of International Trade*, Edward Elgar: Cheltenham UK and Northampton MA, USA.

Bergeijk, P.A.G. van, 2009b, 'Expected extent and potential duration of the world import crunch', *Kyklos*, **62** (4), pp. 479–87.

Bergeijk, P.A.G. van, 2009c, 'I come to bury globalization, not to praise it', Inaugural address, Institute of Social Studies, The Hague, October 29.

Bergeijk, P.A.G. van, 2009d, 'Some Economic Historic Perspectives on the 2009 World Trade Collapse', *ISS Working Paper No. 476*, ISS: The Hague.

Bergeijk, P.A.G. van and J.M. Berk, 2001, 'EMU, the term structure and the Lucas critique', *Kyklos*, **54** (4), pp. 547–56

Bergeijk, P.A.G. van and S. Brakman, 2010, 'Introduction: the come-back of the gravity equation', in: P.A.G. van Bergeijk and S. Brakman (eds), *The Gravity Model in International Trade: Advances and Applications*, Cambridge University Press: Cambridge, pp. 1–26.

Bergeijk, P.A.G. van and D. Kabel, 1993, 'Strategic trade theory and trade policy', *Journal of World Trade*, **27** (6), pp. 175–86.

Bergeijk, P.A.G. van and B.W. Lensink, 1993, 'Trade, capital and the transition in Eastern Europe', *Applied Economics*, **25**, pp. 891–903.

Bergeijk, P.A.G. van and N.W. Mensink, 1997, 'Measuring globalization', *Journal of World Trade*, **31** (3), pp. 159–168.

Bergeijk, P.A.G. van and H. Oldersma, 1990, 'Détente, market-oriented reform and German unification. Potential consequences for the world trade system', *Kyklos*, **43** (4), pp. 599–609.

Bergstrand, J.H. and P. Egger, 2010, 'A general equilibrium theory for estimating gravity equations of bilateral FDI, final goods trade and intermediate trade flows', in: P.A.G. van Bergeijk and S. Brakman (eds), *The Gravity Model in International Trade: Advances and Applications*, Cambridge University Press: Cambridge, pp. 29–70.

Bernard, A.B., S.J. Redding and P.K. Schott, 2008, 'Comparative advantage and heterogeneous firms', *Review of Economic Studies*, **74** (1), pp. 31–66.

Berthou, A. and C. Emlinger, 2009, 'Crisis, Trade Collapse and the Decrease of Import Prices', mimeo, CEPII: Paris.

Bhagwati, J.N. and T.N. Srinivisan, 1976, 'Optimal trade policy and compensation under endogenous uncertainty: the phenomenon of market disruption', *Journal of International Economics*, **6**, pp. 317–36.

Boulhol, H. and A. de Serres, 2010, 'The impact of economic geography on GDP per capita in OECD countries', in: P.A.G. van Bergeijk and S. Brakman (eds), *The Gravity Model in International Trade: Advances and Applications*, Cambridge University Press, pp. 323–54.

Bricogne, J.C., L. Fontagné, G. Gaultier, D. Taglioni and V. Vicard, 2009, 'Firms and the global crisis: French exports in the turmoil', *Vox* (www.voxeu.org), November 5.

Brun, J.-F., C. Carrère, P. Guillaumont and J. de Melo, 2005, 'Has distance died?', *The World Bank Economic Review*, **19** (1), pp. 99–120.

Cairncross F., 1997, *The Death of Distance*, Harvard Business Publications: Cambridge, MA.

Campbell, D.L., D. Jacks, C.M. Meissner and D. Novy, 2009, 'Explaining two trade busts: output vs. trade costs in the Great Depression and today', *Vox* (www.voxeu.org), 19 September.

Cernat, L., 2009, 'An initial assessment of the impact of crisis-driven protectionism on EU trade interests', Paper presented at VNO/NCW, November 12.

Chauffour, J.P. and T. Farole, 2009, 'Trade Finance in Crisis: Market Adjustment or Market Failure?', *World Bank Policy Research Working Paper 5003*, World Bank: Washington DC.

Chauffour, J.P., C. Saborowski and A.I. Soylemezoglu, 2010, 'Trade Finance in Crisis: Should Developing Countries Establish Export Credit Agencies?', *World Bank Policy Research Working Paper 5166*, World Bank: Washington DC.

Cheung, C. and S. Guichard, 2009, 'Understanding the World Trade Collapse', *OECD Economics Departement Working Paper No. 729*, OECD: Paris.

Choi, W.G. and Y. Kim, 2003, 'Trade Credit and the Effect of Macro-financial Shocks: Evidence from U.S. Panel Data', *IMF Working Paper WP03127*, IMF: Washington DC.

Claessens, S., M.A. Kose and M.E. Terrones, 2008, 'What Happens During Recessions, Crunches and Busts?' *IMF Working Paper WP/08/274*, IMF: Washington DC.

CPB, 2009, *CPB-World Trade Monitor*, CPB: The Hague available from: www.cpb.nl/eng/research/sector2/data/trademonitor.html.

Disdier, A. and K. Head, 2008, 'The puzzling persistence of the distance effect on bilateral trade', *Review of Economics and Statistics*, **90**, pp. 37–48.

Dixit, A., 1990, 'Trade policy with imperfect information', in: R.W. Jones and A.O. Krueger (eds), *The Political Economy of International Trade: Essays in Honor of Robert E. Baldwin*, Basil Blackwell: Oxford and Cambridge, MA, pp. 9–24.

Dorsey, T., 2009, 'Trade finance stumbles', *Finance & Development*, **46** (1) pp. 18–19.

Eichengreen, B., 1984, 'Keynes and protection', *The Journal of Economic History*, **44** (2), pp. 363–73

Eichengreen, B. and D. Irwin, 2009, 'The Slide to Protectionism in the Great Depression: Who Succumbed and Why?', *NBER Working paper 15142*, NBER: Cambridge, MA.

Eichengreen, B. and K. O'Rourke, 2009, 'A tale of two depressions', *Vox* (www.voxeu.org), 1 September.

Escaith, H., 2009, 'Trade Collapse, Trade Relapse and Global Production Networks: Supply Chains in the Great Recession' Paper OECD Round Table on Impacts of the Economic Crisis on Globalization and Global Value Chains, Paris, 28 October.

Escaith, H., N. Lindenberg and S. Miroudot, 2010, 'International Supply Chains and Trade Elasticity in Times of Global Crisis', *MPRA Paper 20478*, MPRA: Munich.

Estevadeordal, A., B. Frantz and A.M. Taylor, 2003, 'The rise and fall of world trade, 1870–1939', *Quarterly Journal of Economics*, **118** (2), pp. 359–407.

Evenett, S.J., 2009, 'What can be Learned from Crisis-era Protectionism: An Initial Assessment', *CEPR Discussion Paper Series No. 7494*, CEPR: London.

Evenett S.J., 2010, *Will Stabilisation Limit Protectionism?, The 4th GTA Report*, CEPR: London.

Evenett, S.J., B.M. Hoekman and O. Cattaneo (eds), 2009, *The fateful allure of protectionism: Taking Stock for the G8*, World Bank and CEPR; London.

Faber, G. and C. van Marrewijk, 2009, 'De crisis en de schommelende wereldhandel' (The crisis and fluctuations of world trade, in Dutch), *ESB* **94** (4563S), pp. 20–24.

Fingerand, K.M. and L. Schuknecht, 1999, 'Trade finance and financial crises', *WTO Special Studies 3*, WTO: Geneva.

Frankel, J.A., D. Romer and T. Cyrus, 1996, 'Trade and Growth in East Asian Countries: Cause and Effect?' *NBER Working Paper 5732* Cambridge, MA.

Frederico, G. and A. Tena, 1991, 'On the accuracy of foreign trade statistics (1909–1935): Morgenstern revisited', *Explorations in Economic History*, **28**, pp. 259–73.

Freund, C., 2009a, 'Demystifying the collapse in trade', *Vox* (www.voxeu.org), 3 July.

Freund, C, 2009b, 'The Trade Response to Global Downturns: Historical Evidence', *Policy Research Working Paper 5015*, World Bank: Washington DC.

Friedman, T.L., 2005, *The World is Flat*, Penguin: London.

G20 Trade Finance Expert Group, 2009, 'G20 Trade Finance Experts Group August Report – US–UK Chair's Recommendations for Finance Ministers', available from www.g20.org.

Giovanni, J. di and A.A. Levchenko, 2009, 'Putting the Parts Together: Trade, Vertical Linkages and Business Cycle Comovement', mimeo, University of Michigan: Michigan.

Goldstein, J., 1986, 'The political economy of trade: institutions of protection', *American Political Science Review*, **80** (1), pp. 161–84.

Guttentag, J.M. and R.J. Herring, 1986, 'Dysaster myopia in international banking', *Essays in International Finance 164*, Princeton University Press: Princeton.

Hong, K., J.-W. Lee and H.C. Tang, 2009, 'Crises in Asia: Historical Perspectives and Implication', *ADB Working Papers Series 152*, Asian Development Bank: Manilla.

Huisman, S. and R. Lensink, 2009, 'Microfinanciering en de financiële crisis' (Micro credits and the Financial crisis, in Dutch), mimeo, Landbouw Universiteit Wageningen: Wageningen

Iacovone, L and V. Zavacka, 2009a, Banking Crises and Exports: Lessons from the Past', *World Bank Policy Research Working Papers 5015*, World Bank: Washington DC.

Iacovone, L and V. Zavacka, 2009b, 'Banking crises and exports: Lessons from the past for the recent trade collapse', in: R. Baldwin (ed.), *The Great Trade Collapse: Causes, Consequences and Prospects*, Centre for trade and economic integration, Graduate institute Geneva: Geneva, pp. 107–14.

International Monetary Fund, 2003, *Trade Finance in Financial Crisis: Assessment of Key Issues*, IMF: Washington DC.

International Monetary Fund, 2009a, *World Economic Outlook*, IMF: Washington DC.

International Monetary Fund, 2009b, *World Economic Outlook Update – Contractionary Forces Receding But Weak Recovery Ahead*, IMF: Washington DC.

International Monetary Fund, 2009c, 'IMF Executive Board Concludes 2009 Article IV Consultation with the People's Republic of China', *Public Information Notice (PIN) No. 09/87*, July 22, 2009.

International Monetary Fund–Banking Association For Trade, 2009, *Trade Finance Survey: A Survey Among Banks Assessing the Current Trade Finance Environment*, Fimetrix.

Jacks, D., C.M. Meisner and D. Novy, 2009, 'The role of trade costs in the great trade collapse', *Vox* (www.voxeu.org), November 27.

Jaggers, K. and T.R. Gurr, 1995, 'Tracking democracy's third wave with the Polity III data', *Journal of Peace Research,* **32** (4), pp. 469–82.

Keynes, J.M., 1986, *The General Theory of Employment, Interest and Money*, Collected Writings VII, Macmillan (First published in 1936).

Keynes, J.M., 1984, *The Economic Consequences of the Peace*, Collected Writings II, London: Macmillan (First published in 1919).

Kindleberger, C.P., 1973, *The World in Depression 1929–1939*, Allen Lane The Penguin Press: London.

Kindleberger, C.P., 1978, *Manias, Panics and Crashes: A History of Financial Crises*, MacMillan: London and Basingstoke.

Kofman, P., J.-M. Viaene and C.G. de Vries, 1990, 'Primary commodity prices and exchange-rate volatility', in L.A. Winters and D. Sapsford, (eds), *Primary Commodity Prices: Economic Models and Policy*, Cambridge University Press: Cambridge MA, pp. 213–32.

Kravis, I.B., A. Heston and R. Summers, 1982, *World Product and Income: International Comparisons of Real Gross Product*, United Nations International Comparisons Project Phase III: Baltimore.

Laeven, L. and F. Valencia, 2008, 'Systemic Banking Crises: A New Database', *IMF Working Paper WP/08/224*, IMF: Washington DC.

Lane, P.R. and G.M. Milesi-Ferretti, 2010, 'The Cross-Country Incidence of the Global Crisis', Paper prepared for the IMF/Banque de France/PSE Conference on 'Economic Linkages, Spillovers and the Financial Crisis'.

Leeuwe, G.M. van, 2009, 'Do Changes in Credit Availability Lead to Short-run Deviations from the Long-run Growth Rate in Trade', MA thesis Utrecht School of Economics and Rabo Bank (Kennis en Economisch Onderzoek): Utrecht.

Leeuwe, G.M. and A. Bruinshoofd, 2009, 'Implosie wereldhandel niet door beperkte kredietverlening' (Implosion world trade not caused by credit reductions, in Dutch), *Economisch Statistische Berichten*, **94** (4574), pp. 742–5.

Lehman, J.P., 2008, *If the Global Financial Crisis Becomes a Global Trade Crisis*, IMD: Lausanne.

Levchenko, A.A., L.T. Lewis and L.L. Tesar, 2009, 'The Collapse of International Trade During the 2008–2009 Crisis: In Search of a Smoking Gun', Paper prepared for the IMF/Banque de France/PSE Conference on 'Economic Linkages, Spillovers and the Financial Crisis'.

Lewer, J.J. and H. van den Berg, 2003, 'How large is international trade's effect on economic growth', *Journal of Economic Surveys*, **17** (3), pp. 363–96.

Linden, G., K.L. Kraemer and J. Dedrick, 2007, *Who Captures Value in a Global Innovation System? The case of Apple's iPod*, Personal Computing Industry Center (PCIC): North Irvine CA.

Linders, G.-J., 2006, 'Intangible Barriers to Trade', PhD. Thesis, Vrije Universiteit: Amsterdam.

Lucas, R.E., 1976, 'Econometric policy evaluation: a critique', in: R.E. Lucas (ed.), *Studies in Business-Cycle Theory*, MIT Press: Cambridge MA, pp. 104–30.

Maddison, A., 1985, *Two Crises: Latin America and Asia 1929–38 and 1973–83*, OECD: Paris.

Maddison, A., 1995, *Monitoring the World Economy 1820–1992*, OECD: Paris.

Maddison, A., 2001, *The World Economy: A Millennial Perspective*, OECD: Paris.

Madsen, J.B., 2001, 'Trade barriers and the collapse of world trade during the Great Depression', *Southern Economic Journal*, **67** (4), pp. 848–68.

Marer, P., 1985, *Dollar GNPs of the USSR and Eastern Europe*, Johns Hopkins University Press, Baltimore.

Marrewijk, C. van, 2009, 'Spatial diffusion of technology and the trade collapse', Inaugural address, Utrecht University, November 9.

Marrewijk, C. van and P.A.G. van Bergeijk, 1990, 'Trade uncertainty and specialization: social versus private planning', *De Economist*, **138** (1), pp. 15–32.

Marrewijk, C. van and P.A.G. van Bergeijk, 1993, 'Endogenous trade uncertainty: why countries may specialize against comparative advantage', *Regional Science and Urban Economics*, **23** (4), pp. 681–94.

Mayda, A.M. and D. Rodrik, 2005, 'Why are some people (and countries) more protectionist than others', *European Economic Review*, **49**, pp. 1393–430.

McLaren, J., 2000, '"Globalization" and vertical structure', *American Economic Review*, **90** (5), pp. 1239–54.

Melgar, N., J. Milgram and M. Rossi, 2009, 'The Role of Macroeconomic Performance in Individual's Attitudes Towards Protectionim' *Documento 08/09*, Decon, Univerita da Republica: Granada.

Melitz, M., 2003, 'The impact of trade on intra-industry reallocations and aggregate industry productivity', *Econometrica*, **71**, pp. 1695–725.

Milner, H.V. and K. Kubota, 2005, 'Why the move to free trade? democracy and trade policy in the developing countries', *International Organization*, **59** (1), pp. 107–43.

Miroudot, S. and A. Ragoussis, 2009, 'Vertical Trade, Trade Costs and FDI', *OECD Trade Policy Paper 89*, OECD: Paris.

Mora, J. and W. Powers, 2009, 'Did trade credit problems deepen the great trade collapse?', in: R. Baldwin (ed.), *The Great Trade Collapse: Causes, Consequences and Prospects*, Centre for Trade and Economic Integration, Graduate Institute Geneva: Geneva, pp. 115–25.

Morgenstern, O., 1950, *On the Accuracy of Economic Observations*, Princeton University Press: Princeton.

Moro Visconti, R., 2009, 'Global Recession and Microfinance in Developing Countries: Threats and Opportunities' (24 March), Mimeo, Università Cattolica del Sacro Cuore: Milano: available at SSRN: http://ssrn.com/abstract=1318581.

OECD, 2007, *Economic Outlook 82*, OECD: Paris, December.

OECD, 2008a, *Economic Outlook 83*, OECD: Paris, June.

OECD, 2008b, *Economic Outlook 84*, OECD: Paris, December.

OECD, 2009a, *Economic Outlook, Interim report*, OECD: Paris, March.

OECD, 2009b, *Economic Outlook 85*, OECD: Paris, June.

OECD, 2009c, *Economic Outlook 86*, OECD: Paris, November.

OECD, 2009d, 'Vertical specialization and global value chains', Working Party on International Trade in Goods and Trade in Services Statistics *STD/SES/WPTGS(2009)16/ANN*, OECD Statistics Directorate: Paris.

OECD, 2010, 'Donors' mixed aid performance for 2010 sparks concern', http://www.oecd.org/document/20/0,3343,en_2649_34447_44617556_1_ 1_1_37413,00.html, February 17.

O'Rourke, K., 2006, 'Democracy and Protectionism' *IIIS Discussion Paper 191*, Institute for International Integration Studies: Dublin.

O'Rourke, K., 2009, 'Collapsing trade in a Barbie world', *Irish Economy,* 18 June.

O'Rourke, R.H. and R. Sinnott, 2001, 'The Determinants of Individual Trade Policy Preferences: International Survey Evidence', mimeo, Trinity College: Dublin.

Peels, R., M. Udenio, J.C. Fransoo, M. Wolfs and T. Hendrikx, 2009, 'Responding to the Lehman Wave: Sales Forecasting and Supply Management during the Credit Crisis', *BETA Working Paper Series 297*, TUE: Eindhoven.

Pomery, J., 1984, 'Uncertainty in trade models', in: R.W. Jones and P.B. Kenen, (eds), *Handbook of International Economics*, Amsterdam: North-Holland, pp. 419–65.

Porter, M.E., 1990, *The Competitive Advantage of Nations*, New York: Free Press.

Reich, R.B., 1991, *The Work of Nations: Preparing Ourselves for 21st Century Capitalism*, New York: Vintage Books.

Reinhart, C.M. and K.S. Rogoff, 2009, 'The Aftermath of Financial Crises', *NBER Working Paper 14656*, NBER: Cambridge, MA.

Robertson, R., 2009, 'Mexico and the great trade collapse', *Vox* (www.voxeu.org), 27 November.

Rodrik, D. 2009, 'Growth After the Crisis', mimeo, Harvard Kennedy School, Cambridge, MA, 12 May.

Rothermund, D., 1996, *The Global Impact of The Great Depression 1929–1939*, Routledge: London and New York.

Ruffin, R.J., 1974, 'International trade under uncertainty', *Journal of International Economics*, **4**, pp. 243–59.

Schumpeter, J.A., 1954, *The History of Economic Analysis*, Allen & Unwin: London.

Segura-Cayuela, R. and J.M. Vilarrubia, 2008, 'Uncertainty and Entry into Export Markets' , *Banco de Esapaña Documentos de Trabajo 0811*, Madrid: Banco de España

Serrano, A., 2007, 'Phase transition in the globalization of trade', *Journal of Statistical Mechanics*, p. L01002.

Taleb, N.N., 2007, *The Black Swan: The Impact of the Highly Improbable*, Penguin: London.

Tanaka, K., 2009, 'Trade collapse and vertical foreign direct investment', *VOX* (www.voxeu.org), 7 May.

Tinbergen, J., 1933, *De Konjunktuur* ('The business-cycle', in Dutch), Arbeiderspers: Amsterdam.

Thomas, A., 2009, 'Financial Crises and Emerging Market Trade', *IMF Staff Position Note SPN/09/04*, IMF: Washington DC.

UNCTAD, 2009a, Press note, June 24.

UNCTAD, 2009b, *World Investment Prospects Survey 2009–2010*, UNCTAD: New York and Geneva.

UNCTAD 2009c, *World Investment Report 2009*, UNCTAD: New York and Geneva.

UNCTAD 2009d, *Global Investment Trends Monitor* Nr 1, UNCTAD: Geneva.

UNCTAD, 2009e, 'Keeping ODA afloat: no stone unturned', *UNCTAD Policy Briefs 7,* UNCTAD: New York and Geneva.

UN Economic and Social Council, 2008, 'FDI statistics, the problem or the solution in measuring globalisation?', Note by the Netherlands Central Bank, *ECE/CES/2008/14*, Economic Commission for Europe: Paris.

United Nations Statistical Office, 1962, *International Trade Statistics 1900–1960*, UN: New York.

Vukmanic, F.G., M.R. Czinkota and D.A. Ricks, 1985, 'National and international problems and solutions in the empirical analysis of intra-industry direct foreign investment', in: A. Erdileck (ed.), *Multinational Invaders: Intra-industry Direct Foreign Investment*, St Martins: New York, pp. 160–84.

Wagner, J., 2007, 'Exports and productivity: a survey of the evidence from firm level data', *The World Economy*, **30** (1), pp. 60–82.

Welzenis, G. van and W. Suyker, 2005, 'Explanatory Note on the CPB World Trade Series', *CPB Memorandum 116,* CPB Netherlands Bureau for Economic Policy Analysis, CPB: The Hague.

World Bank, 2009a, *Global Economic Prospects 2009*, Forecast Update, World Bank: Washington DC, March 30.

World Bank, 2009b, *Global Development Finance: Charting a Global Recovery*, World Bank: Washington DC.

World Bank 2009c, *Swimming Against the Tide: How Developing Countries are Coping with the Global Crisis*, World Bank: Washington DC.

World Trade Organization, 2007, *World Trade Report 2007: Six Decades of Multilateral Trade Cooperation: What Have We Learned?*, WTO: Geneva.

World Trade Organization, 2009a, Press note 24 March.

World Trade Organization, 2009b, Press note 22 July.

World Trade Organization, 2009c, *World Trade Report 2009 – Trade Policy Commitments and Contingency Measures*, WTO: Geneva.

Yakop, M. and P.A.G. van Bergeijk, 2009, 'The Weight of Economic and Commercial Diplomacy', *ISS Working Paper 478*, ISS: The Hague.

Index